Training Your Boxer

Second Edition

Joan Hustace Walker

Important Note

This book tells the reader how to train a Boxer. The author and the publisher consider it important to point out that the advice given in the book is meant primarily for normally developed puppies from a good breeder—that is, dogs of excellent physical health and good character.

Anyone who adopts a fully grown dog should be aware that the animal has already formed its basic impressions of human beings. There are dogs that as a result of bad experiences with humans behave in an unnatural manner or may even bite. Only people that have experience with dogs should take in such an animal.

Even well-behaved and carefully supervised dogs sometimes do damage to someone else's property or cause accidents. It is, therefore, in the owner's interest to be adequately insured against such eventualities, and we strongly urge all dog owners to purchase a liability policy that covers their dog.

© Copyright 2012, 2001 by Joan Hustace Walker

All inquiries should be addressed to:
Barron's Educational Series, Inc.
250 Wireless Boulevard
Hauppauge, NY 11788
www.barronseduc.com

ISBN: 978-0-7641-4600-8
Library of Congress Catalog Card No. 2011018223

Library of Congress Cataloging-in-Publication Data
Walker, Joan Hustace, 1962–
   Training your boxer / Joan Hustace Walker.—2nd ed.
     p. cm. — (Training your dog series)
   Includes bibliographical references and index.
   ISBN 978-0-7641-4600-8 (pbk.)
   1. Boxer (Dog breed)—Training. I. Title.
SF429.B75W362   2011
636.73—dc23   2011018223

Printed in China
9 8 7 6 5 4 3 2 1

About the Author

Joan Hustace Walker has been writing professionally since 1984. She is a member of the American Society of Journalists and Authors, the Dog Writers Association of America, and the National Press Photographers Association. Her other book titles include *The Boxer Handbook*. She has had hundreds of articles published by a variety of magazines, including *Modern Maturity*, *Family Circle*, and *Dog World*. Walker's work has received more than 30 national nominations and awards, including seven Maxwell Awards from the Dog Writers Association of America, and the 2009 Responsible Dog Owner's Award from the American Kennel Club. She has been active in the dog fancy for more than 30 years— exhibiting, training, and competing with dogs from the Working, Hound, and Toy Groups.

Acknowledgments

This book would not have been possible without the generous help and experience of two extraordinary Boxer trainers, Tracy Hendrickson (Sunchase Boxers) of Tulsa, Oklahoma and Norbert Zawatzki of Waldsolms, Germany. Also, a special thank you to the talented members of the Boxer training club in Wetzlar, Germany, and Cathy Hubert-Markos (Bachbett Boxers) of Mindoro, Wisconsin.

Cover Credits

Barbara Augello: front cover; Shutterstock: back cover, inside front cover, inside back cover.

Photo Credits

Seth Casteel: pages 20, 70; Dreamstime: pages 24, 122, 138; Jeanmfogle.com: page 75; Tracy Hendrickson: pages viii, 2, 15, 26, 27, 30, 31, 34, 35, 37, 49, 77, 87 (bottom right), 132, 133, 135, 141, 145, 153, 154, 162; Cathy Hubert Markos: pages 4, 7, 9, 18 (top right), 47, 52, 136, 146, 157, 159; Oh My Dog! Photography: page i; Shutterstock: pages 66, 78, 79, 128; Joan Hustace Walker: pages ix, x, xii, 3, 6, 8, 11, 12, 14, 16, 17, 18 (bottom left), 21, 22, 29, 33, 38, 40, 44, 48, 50, 53, 54, 56, 57, 58, 61, 64, 69, 72, 80, 82, 83, 84, 85, 86, 87 (top left), 90, 91, 92, 95, 96, 98, 100 (top left, top right, bottom right), 102, 104, 106, 107, 109, 110, 112, 113 (top, bottom), 115, 116, 119, 120, 124, 126, 131 (left, right), 139, 140, 143, 147, 148, 151, 155, 156.

Contents

Foreword

My one wish, as the founder and chairperson of the American Boxer Rescue Association (ABRA) would be for *every* Boxer owner to read this book and train their Boxers. If this could happen, it would make Boxer Rescue obsolete.

Why? Because the main reason Boxers are turned in to shelters is for behavior problems. These abandoned dogs aren't truly "bad," they just haven't received the attention, love, and training that are required to mold *any* Boxer into a respected, civilized canine that the whole family can enjoy.

In this updated, completely revised 2nd edition of *Training Your Boxer*, Joan Hustace Walker takes readers step-by-step to help them train their Boxers to become treasured family pets. The author also provides insights into what is going on in the Boxer's brain and its many modes of activity. This new edition includes updated training methods that are not only specific to the Boxer but use a variety of positive techniques, including luring, shaping, targeting, and capturing. The book also captures and explains the nuances of combining gentle forms of negative reinforcements (i.e., withholding praise or treats, voice corrections, leash tugs, etc.) with positive reinforcement training techniques to make a truly well-rounded and cutting-edge training manual for beginners.

And, perhaps best of all, *Training Your Boxer* is written in a style that is lively, interesting, and down-to-earth. The author relates as well to Boxer owners as she does to Boxers!

All Boxers deserve to be loved and enjoyed, and *Training Your Boxer* shows readers how to accomplish this task in a fun-filled way. The additional information on activities and performance events shows the depth at which this breed can compete, and may even spark your interest in a new direction with your Boxer.

However far you decide to take your Boxer in his training, there is just one book you should purchase before or after your Boxer arrives home—*Training Your Boxer*. The Boxer ownership road is full of bumps and curves along the way, but with a good roadmap, you're less likely to get lost.

Tracy Hendrickson
Sunchase Boxers
(In nearly 40 years of training, Tracy has been the owner/trainer of more than 35 Boxers, compiling numerous national wins and more than 300 AKC and UKC working dog titles.)

For more than 20 years, I have owned, trained, and bred Boxers. In that time, I also have been deeply interested in all literature that is available on the Boxer. I am delighted with this new book from Joan Hustace Walker. She writes very clearly and in great detail about the Boxer, beginning with the history of the breed and going all the way to the games they play and the training they require.

Training Your Boxer is a great book for a Boxer lover. I met the author in Wetzlar, Germany, a little while ago and I had the opportunity to show her the training we use with German Boxers. I am very honored that some of the information I provided is in this book.

Of course, every time you train a Boxer, you learn something new. We have a saying here in Germany: "All roads lead to Rome—you just need to find the correct one." The road I chose five years ago, always to emphasize the positive, has

enabled me to have the success I now have with my Boxers. Operant training also enables me to begin training with Boxers at an early age. The highest principle is never to use force.

With these training principles, I have been able to achieve early results with my two-year-old Boxer, Henry.

I wish all readers great pleasure in reading this interesting book and much success in practicing the methods this book describes.

Norbert Zawatzki
Director of Training
Boxer Klub e.v. Sitz Munchen

Preface

The Boxer is a wonderful breed. There is no question that the Boxer is and has been one of the most popular breeds—not only in the U.S. and Canada, but worldwide. He is intelligent, energetic, loyal, and handsome—and if these qualities don't win you over, his naturally gregarious temperament and penchant for fun *will*.

The Boxer, however, was bred first and foremost as an active, strong, working breed. Even generations as a pet, show dog, and agility whiz have not dampened much of the Boxer's inherent qualities that made him such a stellar working dog generations ago.

With no training the Boxer's natural instincts and behaviors quickly can create turmoil in the home.

Unfortunately, there is no one magic way to train a Boxer. Though many training books tout "the way" to train *all* dogs, this really isn't possible—especially for the Boxer. Why? First of all, because the Boxer as a breed is very different to train than a retriever, a hound, or a toy. Secondly, within the Boxer breed itself, you will find a variety of temperaments and abilities, and therefore every Boxer will respond to training differently. And finally, all trainers and owners are different, from the way we talk and walk, to our mannerisms, athleticism, patience, and even our ability to *read* what our dogs are thinking. This means that every *person* trains dogs a little differently and some methods are easier for them to use than others.

This combination of variables with the breed, the dogs themselves, and the owners means that there is no cookie cutter way to deal with training every single Boxer. If, however, the Boxer owner is given a variety of training tools and strategies to work with that have been proven to be successful with most Boxers, the owner has an arsenal of training tools from which he or she can determine what works best for his or her particular Boxer.

Training Your Boxer seeks to present Boxer owners with a variety of training strategies and to unravel some of the mysteries involved in training the Boxer. The book takes a look at the psyche of this great canine in order to help explain why he does what he does, and what an owner needs to do to shape these behaviors in a positive way. Interspersed throughout the book you also will find a new feature: "Tracy's Tips." These tips are from renowned Boxer trainer Tracy Hendrickson and highlight some of the finer points of training Boxers, as well as Boxer behavior.

I hope you enjoy working your way through this book as much as I have enjoyed writing it. It has been a great pleasure to work with some of the top Boxer trainers in the United States and Germany for tips and successful strategies. Without their generosity and desire to help Boxer owners everywhere, this book would not have been possible.

1 *Why Train Your Boxer?*

Boxers are great dogs. They're intelligent and athletic, and they love their people. What other breed will routinely do the full-body wiggle dance when she greets you at the door? It is no wonder that the Boxer is one of the most popular breeds in the United States and Canada, as well as many other areas of the world.

The Boxer, however, needs training in order to become a treasured family pet. This breed is an extremely muscular and powerful dog with boundless enthusiasm and energy. An untrained, unsocialized, full-grown Boxer cannot only wreak havoc at home, but also in the neighborhood. (Not intentionally, of course!)

It is almost always the Boxer that has had no training that ends up banished to the backyard because her owners can't handle an unbridled, uncontrollable 60-pound (27-kg) whirlwind of solid muscle in the house. Once in the back-yard, the Boxer becomes even more miserable because she is separated from the family she loves. Other undesirable habits quickly crop up, such as pulling the back door off its hinges to get back inside, scratching furiously, or barking for attention; when that fails, efforts are often turned toward digging and jumping fences.

Usually, it is not too long after the Boxer has been cast out to the backyard that the family gives up entirely on the dog and turns her into the shelter. What is truly sad is that this whole scenario can be avoided with early and consistent training, as well as with an owner who can meet the Boxer's needs for mental and physical challenges.

Of course, you already understand the importance and need for training because you are holding this book. Just in case you need some additional ammunition to solidify your belief that training is a good thing for both you and your Boxer, read on.

Advantages of a Well-trained Dog

1. **There Is Less Chaos.** If a dog is left to her own ways, she will fall back on the only things she knows—canine behavior or "dog ways." When living with a family, these behaviors are generally unacceptable. Marking the kitchen table, bowling over kids, and grabbing the roast off the serving plate are all examples of behaviors that are acceptable to

forward to and needs. Training sessions also give you an opportunity to exercise your Boxer. And, training with positive reinforcement-based methods will establish your leadership with her in a gentle, nonconfrontational manner. All of this helps to develop the Boxer's place in the family as a loyal and trusted pet, and results in a well-balanced dog.

4. Training Creates a Dog That Is a Joy With Which to Live. A dog that will sit while waiting to be served her food, walk without pulling on a leash, and come when she is called (the first time), is a great house pet. Teaching the basic skills of living will develop a Boxer that understands the rules of the house and will not try to challenge you or your family.

5. Training Helps Your Dog Gain Respect from Fearful or Reserved Neighbors. Though the Boxer continues to have a reputation as a well-tempered dog and not a breed prone toward unprovoked aggression, many people judge the Boxer by looks alone. The short nose, cropped ears, and impressive-looking jaw can evoke a wary if not fearful reaction from many people. For this reason, the Boxer owner has an added responsibility to present this breed as a well-trained, congenial dog. If the neighbors are impressed with your dog's impeccable manners while on walks, you're likely to never receive any complaints. However, if she drags you uncontrollably down the street barking loudly (even if it's because she wants to play), your neighbors may voice concerns about your "vicious" dog. Totally unfair,

dogs, but not to their human families. Training your Boxer gives you the tools to develop a well-behaved dog that is eager to please you and abide by your rules—or at least most of them.

2. Training Identifies and Reduces Behavior Problems. If you begin training your Boxer puppy at a very early age, you will be more in tune with your Boxer. If there are any potential behavior problems, you will be able to identify them early and prevent them from becoming a behavior that has been allowed to exist for many years. A long-term behavior is much more difficult to modify.

3. Training Develops a Well-balanced Boxer, Emotionally and Physically. The Boxer is truly a "people" dog and thrives on attention. Regular training gives you the quality time she looks

yes, but it is best to train her to be an exemplary ambassador for the breed.

6. **Training Deepens the Human-dog Bond.** The more you work with your Boxer, the deeper your bond will be with her. Studies have shown, too, that owners who spend time training their dogs and who compete in activities, tend to share their successes with their dogs. They become partners, a team, working toward a common goal. Positive relationships between dogs and their owners are ones in which the owner may reap considerable benefits, too, such as a longer life, better health, and quicker recovery from surgery, to name a few.

7. **Training Establishes Children as "Leaders."** If you have children, involving them in the day-to-day training of your Boxer will help her to understand that these little people with the high voices are "masters," too, rather than puppies, playmates, or chew toys. Methods for teaching her to willingly accept commands and handling from your children are included in Chapter 8: Seven Basic Commands (see Involving the Kids, page 108).

Giving a Working Dog a Job to Do

Because the Boxer is truly a working breed, the benefits of training go a step further. The Boxer was bred to work closely with her handler (see History of the Boxer, page 5), and as a working breed, these innate characteristics are still very much a part of the Boxer. Give this breed a job to do and she will relish the opportunity to work with you. But what sort of job can you give this dog?

Training your Boxer new skills, such as basic or advanced obedience, agility, carting, or tracking, for instance, can give your Boxer a real purpose for all her training. If you have the time, becoming involved in an activity in which your Boxer is apt to excel can further develop her. You will notice a difference in her heightened responses to you in everyday life, too. Don't fret however, if you don't have time for a dog sport. Your Boxer will be completely happy to take on any job you might assign her, such as the enviable position of being "chief ball retriever" or "primary jogging companion."

2 *Understanding the Boxer*

As mentioned in the previous chapter, Boxers are working dogs. Since the inception of the breed, the Boxer has been bred to work in a variety of jobs, all of which included working with his handler.

History of the Boxer

The Boxer was one of the very first breeds recognized by Germany as a police dog in the early 1920s. In order to earn this recognition, breeders had to show the dog's proficiency at performing a variety of tasks, including obeying basic commands, tracking, and protection work. These tests were the basis for today's Schutzhund tests. The Boxer was so proficient at this work that as a breed it had the greatest percentage of members pass the tests, second only to the Airedale.

War dogs. During both World War I and World War II, Boxers served in a variety of war dog positions, including the role of a guard dog trained to prevent prisoners from passing messages to civilians, and a patrol dog that would alert his handler to danger or help the soldier find his way from one location to another along dangerous and dark routes. Boxers were also used to run messages through battle-torn fields and under heavy fire. As an ambulance dog, the Boxer was used to find wounded soldiers and lead medics back to the wounded. (One Boxer received Germany's Iron Cross for saving so many lives during World War I.)

Service dogs. After the wars, Boxers continued to be used in a variety of close-working service jobs in both the United States and Europe. Today, in the United States, Boxers are used as service dogs for the disabled, and as trained animal-assisted therapy dogs. A growing number of handlers are using Boxers quite successfully as Search and Rescue (SAR) dogs. A select group of trainers in the northern midwest states are experiencing amazing success with Boxers as K9s trained for both patrol work and drug detection. (For more information on these stellar working dogs, see contact information for the United States Boxer Association, page 160). In Europe, Boxers are used as guide dogs for the blind, and frequently are trained by volunteer organizations and the Red Cross in search and rescue work.

Police dogs. In the Boxer's home country, he is still listed as one of Germany's accepted breeds for police work; however, the German Shepherd and the Belgian

Malinois are far more popular today. There's a common saying in Germany among K-9 officers: "In the time it takes to train one Boxer, an officer can train two German Shepherds." This is usually recanted with a smile and a shake of the head, and a further comment on the Boxer not being too serious about his tasks or "having too many jokes in his head." However, all this is noted with the qualifier that if an officer chooses to train a Boxer, perhaps because he or she has had experience with the breed, the *trained* police Boxer is a very good dog to have.

The key here is *trained*. Even among those who are experienced in training working dogs, the Boxer can still prove to be a challenge. For those who live, breathe, and *know* Boxers, the task may still be time consuming, but it is much simpler and extremely rewarding. The trick therefore, is to *understand* the Boxer.

Innate Instincts

For generations, the Boxer was selectively bred for *specific* working dog characteristics. Along with these working characteristics, there are also a few traits that are just, well, "pure" Boxer. Armed with a knowledge of working dog and pure Boxer traits, you will be better equipped to understand your own dog and modify your training methods to match his needs.

The following are some traits that are commonly associated with the Boxer breed.

High activity level/energy. The Boxer was bred for endurance. It was at one time expected to work beside its owner all day or as long as it was needed. Even today in Germany, one of the prerequisites for breeding is that the Boxer is able to display this working trait of endurance. As part of the German breeding suitability test (which includes health tests, a passing conformation rating, and a performance test), the Boxer must be able to trot alongside a bicycle for roughly 12 miles (19 km) with only a few brief breaks.

So, what does this mean to the Boxer owner who is trying to train his or her dog? It means that you are working with a dog that has a healthy activity level. The Boxer is an extremely flashy, agile, and quick-footed dog when trained, but this breed can be a challenge to get focused as a young puppy or as an adolescent. To make training sessions more productive with younger Boxers, you must therefore consider your timing carefully. A brief romp to help blow off some steam could be just what it takes to get an energetic Boxer to concentrate on the task at hand; however, too much exercise and he may become too tired to focus on learning.

Strength. The Boxer is an incredibly strong animal. He was originally bred to excel in work that requires raw, physical strength, such as protection work, in which the dog is trained to bite a padded "helper" (a man in a protective suit) on command and not let go until given the command to release. The ability to hold onto a full-grown man is impressive enough, but to have the strength to be able to hold the man and keep him from running away takes an incredibly strong dog. The Boxer is this dog.

With this kind of strength, a pet Boxer can easily drag his owner down the street if he is not taught to walk without pulling. He can also, as an adult, literally use his strength to avoid doing anything he doesn't want to do, which is a problem with the dog that is not trained to obey your commands. Fortunately, Boxers are eager learners and want to please; they can learn virtually anything with gentle, positive reinforcement training (see Approaches to Training, page 15). If you use the right techniques, you'll be able to channel your Boxer's strength into very positive activities.

Courage. The Boxer is noted for his great courage. The Boxer was bred to be

a self-confident breed that could be both brave in the face of the most fearsome threat, and yet gentle and kindhearted with those he loves. Today, there is a range of temperaments among Boxers, with many still possessing this intrinsic courage and a natural instinct to guard their loved ones, home, and territory. There are also those that appear to be so outgoing that it is generally assumed they would lead a burglar to the jewels just to make friends. Don't let this wonderful outward appearance fool you. The friendly, confident dog is perhaps the best guardian of all. Your Boxer can be trusted with everyone but will know when you are truly threatened.

Every once in a while, you will find a Boxer that is fearful or timid. This can be a result of either an inherited temperament or poor early life experiences, such as lack of socialization. Or it could be a combination of both genetics and environment. Whatever the reasons for the fearfulness, this Boxer will need an experienced hand and some extra nurturing from the owner to provide an environment that will help develop him into a more self-assured dog.

Many of these Boxers, once they learn to trust humans again and overcome any other fears they might have, can become excellent pets and even good competitors.

If your Boxer is a self-confident type and possesses great strength of mind, he is also likely to possess a great will, and this may mean that without guidance, he may think his way of doing things makes more sense than yours. The self-confident, courageous Boxer requires a loving environment with an affirmative, patient owner who is willing to provide the structure and consistent but firm leadership this dog needs.

Intelligence. Combined with the Boxer's self-confidence, strong will, and courage, this breed possesses a great sense of cleverness. What this translates to is that he will remain two steps ahead of anything you can possibly envision. Did you ever think your Boxer would figure out

how to get into the refrigerator? Open a door using a round doorknob? Jump the back fence, run around to the front door, and ring the doorbell? It's pretty much a given that your Boxer will think of several things that you could never have imagined. The Boxer's intelligence at solving problems is impressive. Their intelligence in creating *new* problems is perhaps even *more* impressive. Just when you think you've got your dog to be consistent in his response to a command, watch out! He may think of something new to do, just to toss things up a bit.

For the Boxer owner, this could mean frustrating periods with your pet in which *you* will be mentally taxed on problem solving with him. Maintaining a good sense of humor helps with this aspect of the Boxer, as does a generous dose of patience. It also helps to be familiar with potential Boxer antics while rearing him, so you can at least be close to predicting—and thus preventing—certain training challenges.

Close working. Boxers, as with many German breeds, were bred to work closely with their handlers. They were not intended to be dogs that work independently of their master or at great distances from their handlers. Boxers were developed to assist the handlers in whatever job they were given to do and to be responsive to their masters' commands.

The close-working trait of the Boxer, coupled with his eagerness to please his owner, are good training characteristics to possess. These same traits, however, mean that he will never want to be far from his humans. He was not bred to be a loner; he thrives in the company of people. Therefore, if you cannot spend a lot of time with your pet or involve him in much of your daily activities, you are sure to experience behavior problems, namely the complete and utter destruction of your home and yard. If you work with him and include him in all that you do, you will find his working traits are tremendous assets.

Awareness. As a working dog, the Boxer was bred to recognize *change*. Anything different in the dog's environment—a movement, a sound, a scent—is keenly noted. As a war dog and as a patrol dog today, this quality of heightened awareness is a vital characteristic for the working success of this breed. For the pet owner, the Boxer may appear easily distracted and go on high alert for unfathomable reasons. Over time and with consistent training, the Boxer will still note changes in his environment; however, he will understand how to filter what he senses and create a more appropriate response (i.e., a falling leaf is okay for you to ignore, but the guy hiding behind the bush is *not*).

Clowning. The Boxer separates himself from many of the other working breeds in that he never takes life too seriously—ever. He is known to be a clown during all stages of life, from puppyhood to old age. This irrepressible characteristic of the Boxer knows no boundaries, even international ones. The most highly-titled Schutzhund Boxers in Germany have been known to "do the kidney bean" at the sight of the first person who *might* pet them.

Though this silliness and perpetual puppyhood might frustrate some trainers who expect all work and no play from

---

TRACY'S TIPS

The "death" of an obedience Boxer is boredom. To avoid having a "drag-along" performance by your Boxer, pick up the pace! If you're animated, you Boxer will be, too. Basically, you get what you put into your dog.

their dogs, the true Boxer lover accepts this characteristic as part of the endearing qualities of the Boxer.

Channeling the Positives

With an understanding of how some of the Boxer's inherent traits may affect your training approach, it is equally important to be aware of some common training mistakes that owners sometimes make with their dogs. Though Boxers are working dogs and can be trained for such serious, focused work as advanced obedience, tracking, and protection work, they are not a "hard headed" or a "thick-skinned" breed. Boxers are typically very responsive to their owner's corrections, and a heavy hand can squash their inborn enthusiasm.

Be forewarned: once the joy of training is lost for a Boxer, it is very hard to regain. Therefore, you must take great care to maintain your Boxer's enthusiasm at all times.

This also means that training sessions must be kept interesting and motivating. Though some dogs may willingly sit on command 100 times in a row, or fetch dumbbell toys for hours on end, this repetitive training will only bore your Boxer. When a Boxer becomes bored, watch out! The creativity (or "unlearning") starts.

Training sessions need to be kept brisk and relatively short until your Boxer advances in his training and matures to a level at which he willingly can focus for longer periods of time. Regardless of how long your Boxer physically can train, be cognizant of your pet's mental abili-

ties and always end the training session *before* he becomes bored or tired. Puppies can receive a few minutes of training interspersed throughout the day, whereas an adult may easily be able to focus for 20 minutes or longer, depending on the activity, the level to which the dog is currently trained, and the handler's skill in training.

In general, the Boxer is a wonderful and interesting breed to train. With a good grounding on Boxer behavior and an understanding of typical Boxer traits, you will be well equipped for modeling training methods to best meet your pet's needs.

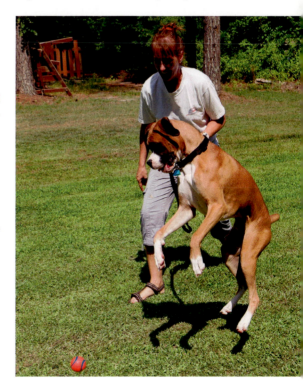

3 How the Boxer Learns

To maximize the efficiency of your training and to minimize as many human errors as possible, it is important to understand a little about what is going on in your Boxer's head. Unfortunately, there is not a "Boxer language dictionary" available for sale—yet. We do know, however, quite a bit about how dogs communicate and learn.

The Concept of Learning from a Dog's View

Your Boxer has a *great* capacity to learn! And, what sets this breed apart from many others, is that she *wants* to learn. She wants to be your companion, your trusted friend, *your* Boxer. Learning the subtleties behind how your Boxer learns what you teach her and how she learns from other dogs can give your training abilities quite a boost.

Visual Communication

Research has shown that dogs are very visual. They are stimulated by what they see. This probably comes as no surprise to Boxer owners who are used to their dogs

spotting and investigating every leaf, airplane, car, child, or any other object that moves. Dogs also look for and respond to visual cues, which means that much of the dog's "language" is visual. Dogs use their muzzles, ears, eyes, tails, and bodies to get their points across. These body cues can communicate a myriad of messages such as contentment, annoyance, submissiveness, and playfulness, as well as fear and aggression.

Hand signals. Your movements are important to your dog. Visual cues such as hand signals are very effective in training dogs. (That's a tremendous plus if you've got a deaf Boxer!) Hand signals also always *sound* the same to a dog. Using hand signals in training, therefore, gives the dog a lot of consistency in training.

For example, if you've chosen to touch your chin for the *sit* command, no matter what kind of mood you are in when you give the command (perhaps grouchy from work or angry because your loving Boxer just polished off your lunch), the command looks and sounds the same. Hand signals also transfer well from person to person: You will find that your five-year-old can give a hand signal and have the dog obey, whereas the higher-pitched voice of a child trying to get a wild ado-

your facial expressions and your body is tense or without much expression, she will quickly realize you are displeased and irritated, which will result in a confused and unhappy dog.

It is also critical to recognize your Boxer's changing body language during training sessions so you can better adjust your approach to training. In particular, be sure to review "Body Language Primer" on page 49 and understand the signs of stress, which is also an indication that your Boxer is confused. Keep her happy, keep training fun, and she will learn more quickly and you will progress as a team much faster.

If you've had a bad day, wait until you're in a better mood to work with your dog. If you tend to be very reserved with your body language, work on smiling more and loosening up—your Boxer won't tell anyone how silly you can be!

lescent dog to sit may only have the effect of exciting the Boxer even more.

Body language. Beyond hand signals, the entire movement and silent language of your body are being watched and interpreted by your dog. For this reason, your body language is very important in training dogs. Your Boxer can see by the way you walk and by the expression on your face *precisely* how you feel, and she will quickly pick up on this mood. If you walk with a bounce, smile, and use your entire body to express your happiness with her, not only will she be more attentive, she will intuitively know she's doing a good job and you are pleased with her—and her mood will mirror *yours*. If, however, you are scowling or stern with

Oral communication. Body language, of course, is not the only tool you can use to train your Boxer. Dogs do learn to understand some of our language and tend to filter out the words that are important or pertain to them.

So how much can our dogs understand of what we are saying? Some psycholo-

TRACY'S TIPS

The most common misconception owners have is that if their Boxer yawns, she is tired. She's not tired! She is stressed. Help her relax. Play with her and then return to training.

gists believe dogs can learn to understand as many different words as a toddler, or roughly 200 spoken words. Still others believe that dogs can learn in excess of 300 words. At a minimum then, there's no reason why a dog can't understand a repertoire of 10 to 20 words that will be the basis for your commands. Of course, getting your Boxer to respond appropriately to these words lies in your training, which we will deal with shortly!

Age Counts

A Boxer owner should also take into consideration the age of his or her dog when training her. The most distinct difference between puppies and adults is that puppies have difficulty focusing on any one thing for very long. Puppies benefit the most from many small, short training sessions or intermittent command work throughout the day (i.e., "*sit*" for a cookie, "*sit*" for her dinner bowl, "*sit*" before the door is opened, "*sit*" for a pat from the neighbor, etc.).

The adult Boxer has overcome a lot of the puppy's hampered ability to focus, but a young adult (12–24 months) can still be easily distracted in training. It's not that the ability to focus isn't there at this age; rather, it goes back to the discussion about the Boxer's intelligence, her natural instincts of heightened awareness, and her tendency to become quickly bored. Learning must remain fast-paced, fun, and creative for any age Boxer. As long as you remain more interesting than the leaf falling from a nearby tree, you've got the situation under control.

Approaches to Training

Now that you know a bit about how your Boxer learns, it's time to learn what kind of training tools you have at your disposal and what works best with the Boxer. So, let's begin with what doesn't work: physical domination.

Physical Domination

Physical domination includes hitting, slapping, beating, pinning, "scruffing" (grabbing the dog by the skin on her neck and getting right into her face), and alpha rolling (forcing the dog into a submissive position on her back). These methods are *not* effective and accomplish nothing except, perhaps, to cause a dog that would never have bitten otherwise to bite in self-defense. *Abuse is not a teaching tool.*

Though they are rapidly disappearing, there are still a few "old school" trainers who will claim physical dominance is the only way to train some dogs; if you find one of these folks, run. Here's why.

Boxers are intelligent, trusting, and loyal creatures. Just like children, dogs can take only so much of any kind of abusive treatment before one of several things happens. The dog may become distrustful of all humans. She could become so fearful of her master that she might actually fear for her life and try to protect herself by biting. (This is not considered dominant behavior.) Or, if the Boxer is a self-assured, dominant type, attempts by an aggressive owner to manhandle the dog into submission will escalate the situation, not solve it. With any of these scenarios, nothing is accomplished. So, let it be said that if there is one way *not* to train a dog, it is with physical domination.

Negative Reinforcement

This type of training does work, but it is not a preferred method for training as a whole.

Technically speaking, negative reinforcement is the use of a verbal or physical correction when the dog makes a mistake. For example, if a dog lunges ahead of the handler, the quick uptake or "pop" of a metal choke chain is a negative reinforcement. The dog realizes quickly that if she lunges forward, she will get hurt—a little. So, by seeking to avoid punishment, this is how she learns.

Verbal negative reinforcement includes shouting *"No"* or *"Stop"* when your puppy starts to urinate on the carpeting. Your voice tells the puppy what you don't want her to do; however, your voice correction doesn't tell your puppy what you *want* her to do. Only your actions following this halting command, such as picking

Negative reinforcement is not necessarily a physical correction—or a "bad" thing. It can be as innocuous as withholding a positive reinforcement such as a treat. An example of an effective negative reinforcement is not putting the food bowl down until the jumping Boxer stands quietly. You are effectively withholding something positive (his dinner) if he is not giving you the behavior you desire (a calm Boxer).

up the puppy and putting her outside, accompanied with praise or a treat, will tell her what you want her to do.

Unfortunately, negative reinforcement—particularly physical methods—lends itself to being a training tool that is often mishandled. Some owners take the corrections too far and are physically abusive with their dogs. Some dogs are so "soft" emotionally that a swift correction (verbal or physical) can literally crush their enthusiasm. Once enthusiasm is lost, it is rarely, if ever, regained.

Negative reinforcement, as mentioned above, can get results, but research has shown that both owners and dogs enjoy positive training methods much more. Additionally, some researchers have shown that positive training methods are generally faster in shaping behaviors and may have a greater rate of retention. More than thirty years of use and continued evolvement have made positive reinforcement the preferred method of training today.

Positive Reinforcement

The key to this popular method of training is to set your dog up for success, limit her chances for failure, and reward her when she does a task correctly.

In the United States, the pioneers credited with developing positive, motivational training methods are veterinarian and animal behaviorist Ian Dunbar and scientist and animal trainer Karen Pryor. Working independently beginning in the 1980s, Dunbar and Pryor are credited not only with presenting their methods of positive, motivational training, but also with being

instrumental in the widespread adoption of this training method by trainers all over the country. The system is based on getting the Boxer to respond with a specific behavior using one of several methods, such as luring, shaping, capturing, or targeting. Once the behavior is given by the dog, a reward is given to reinforce the behavior, and then a word or signal can be associated or linked with the correct behavior.

Four Techniques That Work

Okay, so how exactly do you get a Boxer to do something that wasn't her idea in the first place? Pushing a Boxer into position *may* be possible with a little puppy but is virtually impossible with an adolescent or adult Boxer. (Have you seen the muscles on the Boxer's hind end?) Besides, why use force when there's a much simpler way than wrestling your Boxer to the floor (and most likely losing the struggle)? There are much easier methods! In order to teach a specific behavior, such as the *sit*, you can use any of the following methods—or use them in combination.

Luring. This method is one that most dog owners will use to teach many beginning commands, such as the *sit*. With luring, the owner uses a tasty tidbit or a favorite toy

to physically lure the Boxer into a position. For example, with the *sit*, the lure is held in the owner's hand and is slowly passed from the dog's nose backwards toward her ears. The Boxer naturally rocks backward to follow the treat and will fold into a *sit*. The treat or toy literally lures the dog into the correct position, thus the term "luring." The reward comes when the dog is in position, as does the word/command association—but more on that in a moment.

Shaping. Sometimes it's not as easy to get a Boxer to provide a specific behavior, and the new skill may need to be taught in stages. If this is the case, "shaping" may be an easier way to teach this skill. Basically, it is similar to luring in that a treat, toy, or other "lure" can be used to create the behavior; however, the Boxer is awarded for making progress—she doesn't have

to provide the exact behavior to receive a reward initially. An example when shaping can be used very successfully is in teaching the *down*. Most Boxers won't go completely down on their first attempts to follow a treat to the floor. Often, they *will* go halfway. With shaping, you can reward this effort, release them (see Release Commands, page 99), and try again. (Note: it is important *not* to link any command with the exercise at this point. Doing so might link a crouch with the word *down* rather than a full *down*!) On each try, require your Boxer to make more of an effort and get closer to a real *down* before rewarding her. Continue to reward her, release her, and try again.

When the Boxer finally goes all the way into the *down*, then and only then is the voice command linked with the action.

Capturing. This training technique is often used to teach dogs to do tricks based on behaviors the dog naturally offers. For example, spinning in place, rolling over, barking on command, and other tricks can be taught by catching the dog in the act, so to speak, and linking

Mild corrections (such as a quick—not hard!—pop with the leash) are only effective if a dog knows the command—and knows it very, very well. It is only at this time that the Boxer would have a clue as to why she received a reminder that she was supposed to be doing something. If she doesn't know the command well and receives a correction, this will only lead to increased confusion. In the early stages, it is often better to forgo a correction and lure the dog into the behavior you want. Then, back up your training to reteach the command so that the dog is responding with speed and confidence.

There will come a time, however, in your training when (not if) your Boxer will look at you and not perform the command you've given.

It won't be because she is confused or didn't hear you; it will be because she either doesn't want to or is testing the waters to see if she really has to obey. She does. This is when a gentle, mild, and appropriate correction or consequence is necessary. Remember, negative reinforcement can be such things as: the withholding of praise or a treat, a verbal response (Eh! Eh!), or a tug upward (cue for a sit). If you've been training dogs forever, these consequences come quite naturally; if you haven't been in training for a while, this is when an instructor and a training class can give you some very good guidelines. Most important to remember is that consequences only occur when a Boxer knows—without a doubt—what she is supposed to do.

a voice command or hand signal to the action. This method can also be used to teach commands, such as the *sit* or *down*, too. For example, if your Boxer is starting to turn in circles on her bed and is preparing to lie down, wait until she is starting to finally lie down and then link the voice command ("*Down!*") or a hand signal to the action.

Targeting. This training technique can be used for teaching many skills that might be more difficult to learn with a treat or toy as a lure, such as performing an out and back (where you send your dog away from you) in more advanced levels of obedience, but it can also be used to fine-tune an amazingly sharp *heel* (or even a walk nicely by your side). For this training technique, the Boxer is taught to focus on and follow a "target," which is usually a training tool called a target stick (it looks much like an expandable pointer). To teach a dog to use a target stick, the following technique can be used:

1. Hold out your finger closer to your dog's nose. As soon as she touches your finger, click and treat (or reward with praise and treat). Repeat, repeat, and repeat until she gets the hang of touching your finger for a treat.
2. Introduce the target stick. Hold the target stick in your hand so that it is just slightly an extension of your finger, keeping most of the stick hidden up your arm. Extend your finger to your Boxer as in step one, and reward and treat when she touches the target stick.
3. Extend the target stick slowly. Each time your Boxer touches the end of the target stick, praise and reward her.
4. Introduce the voice command "*Touch.*" Link the word "touch" with your Boxer touching the tip of the target stick. Reward and release her—and repeat this level until she's "got" it.
5. Move the target stick. Now you can start having fun. Move the stick a little

TRACY'S TIPS

If you don't have enthusiasm when you're training, your dog will quit offering new behaviors—she'll quit trying. A more enthusiastic Boxer means you'll have a longer capture period for learning—and a Boxer who will keep trying to get it "right." Likewise, if you keep telling a puppy "no!" she'll shut down. You want to teach your puppy to keep trying, and to do this you need to praise her for giving you new behaviors and then shape the ones you want.

Many positive, motivational training methods use food as both a lure (i.e., to position the dog into a sit) and a reward; however, you may choose to use something different. It really depends on what your Boxer's strongest stimulus is. Is it food? Play? A ball? Your voice? Or, is it physical attention? Perhaps your Boxer will respond best to a combination of rewards, such as food, praise, and pats.

Items that can be used to reward your dog include treats, balls, verbal praise, physical praise, and even playtime with a tug toy. What type of positive reinforcement you use can greatly determine how quickly your dog learns and affect how eager she is to please you. For more information on rewards, see Reinforcements, page 89.

Word and Signal Association

Perhaps the most important part of training is *when* you associate or link the voice command or hand signal with the behavior. If you remember nothing else, remember this: only link the command when you are 99 percent sure the dog will be successful in completing the behavior. When teaching the *sit*, for example, in the beginning you will only say *"sit"* when the dog sits. As she learns and links the verbal command with the action of sitting, back up the verbal command and give it as she's 80 percent into her *sit*.

A common mistake—and one that is frequently taught in beginning obedience classes—is to give the verbal command before the puppy or dog even knows the behavior that is being asked. This produces mass confusion. If you give the

left, a little right, a little up—give her the *touch* command, and reward and release for each correct repetition.

6. Use the stick to teach a skill. Your Boxer is now focused on the stick. You can use this for teaching how to walk nicely by holding the stick's tip where you'd like your Boxer's nose to be. Reward and repeat.

7. Fade the stick. Slowly decrease the length of the stick, and use your finger as the target. Replace this eventually with a hand signal for the command.

verbal command for the *sit* when the Boxer is not all the way into her *sit*—and she doesn't complete her *sit*—you've taught her to crouch when you say "*sit*." When teaching a new behavior, you don't even have to link a voice command with the action until the Boxer is comfortable being lured into position. Once your Boxer lures into position quickly and easily multiple times without hesitating, introduce a voice command *as the Boxer completes the behavior*—in this case, as

the Boxer completes the *sit*. In this way, you avoid teaching your Boxer the wrong behavior accidently.

No Repeat Commands

We've all heard it—the owner looks at his puppy and says "*Sit*," and the Boxer ignores this command and keeps playing around, maybe chewing on her leash. The owner repeats the command "*Sit*" with a little more determination. Nothing from the puppy. The owner now says "*Sit!*" with a hint of frustration. Still no reaction from the puppy. Then the owner shouts "*SIT!*" The puppy now shrinks back a bit, confused and a bit frightened, and she slowly, hesitantly sits.

What has just happened? One, the handler has lost his temper and just took the joy out of this training session. Two, the owner has just taught his Boxer a very bad thing—that the pup doesn't have to sit until the owner has barked out at least four commands for the *sit*. (This mistake happens frequently with the *come* command, too.)

Avoid putting yourself in this position by only giving a command when you've got your Boxer's attention and you're 99

percent sure that your puppy or dog will give you the behavior *and* if you are in a position where if your Boxer doesn't give you the desired behavior, you have the ability to lure her into position.

What if it's too late? You've already given the command for *sit* and your puppy is bouncing around, not in a *sit*. Do not repeat the command. She either heard the command and is ignoring you, or she heard the command and is confused as to what do. Hold her gently by the collar and use a treat or toy to lure her into the *sit*. Reward her. Now, go back and reinforce the sit by luring, linking the command at the end of the *sit*, and rewarding her. Build her back up to a solid, confident response to the *sit* command.

Training the Deaf Boxer

Deafness is part of the Boxer breed. As with other breeds that can have coats of pure white or white with patches of color, the Boxer has a genetic risk for bilateral deafness, or deafness in both ears. This type of deafness is seen in Boxers with white or check (white with patches of color) coats, and is caused by the lack of pigment in the cells lining the dog's ears. There is no known way to correct this hearing loss.

Previously, deaf dogs were often euthanized because it was believed that the deaf dog was untrainable. Not so. And it doesn't take a special trainer, either. All that is needed is a slightly different form of training.

If you own a deaf Boxer, you will be able to teach your dog all the commands

> **TRACY'S TIPS**
> *Deaf dogs do well in homes with a well-trained, hearing dog. The deaf Boxer can signal off the hearing dog by watching his movements. If you don't have a second dog, this would be a good reason to add a dog—just make sure the hearing dog is very well trained and responsive to commands.*

and tricks in this book with one basic variation: The method you will use for gaining your deaf dog's attention will be different. Since she is deaf, she cannot hear her name, the set-up cue used to let the dog know she must listen. The owner of the deaf Boxer must do something different to get the dog's attention: a stomp on the floor, a mild pagerlike buzz of an electronic collar, the flash of a penlight, or the toss of a beanbag across her line of vision.

Once the deaf dog's attention is gained, she is rewarded. Over time, the deaf Boxer will learn the cue to focus on her owner. When she understands the *look at me* signal, the owner can begin coupling this with training for as many commands as desired. The commands can be taught using food lures as outlined in this book coupled with hand signals, rather than voice commands.

Many owners use their own version of hand signals to communicate with their deaf dogs; some choose to use American Sign Language. The choice is really the owner's.

4 *House-training*

To be a successful house dog and a valued companion, your Boxer will need to be dependable in the house. He must learn to relieve himself outside and not in your living room or behind a couch.

Dogs are born with the inherent desire not to soil their dens or immediate sleeping areas. In order to house-train a dog, you must take his innate desire to not soil his bed and transfer this behavior to first one room, then several rooms, and eventually the entire home. This involves a great deal of patience, practice, timing, and consistency. Fortunately, house-training is something all Boxers, regardless of age, should learn readily and with few problems.

Despite this, one of the most frequently heard complaints among dog owners is: "I'm having difficulties house-training my dog!" The fault is rarely with the dog. If a dog is not learning a certain behavior, the problem usually lies with the trainer and not the dog. The same is true of house-training.

When a Boxer does not house-train easily, it is most often because the owner failed the dog in one of four ways: 1) the owner did not understand the basic principles of house-training a young puppy or adult dog; 2) the owner could not meet the house-training needs and schedule of

the Boxer; 3) the owner did not train the Boxer positively and/or with consistency; or 4) the owner did not recognize the distress signals of a Boxer that needs to go outside.

Understanding Urges and Abilities

The good news is that Boxers are noted for their ability to house-train at an early age. They tend to be meticulous in wanting to keep their living area clean, which is the key to successful house-training. Some owners even refer to the Boxer's cleanliness as "catlike." The Boxer puppy begins to show this inherent fastidiousness as early as five weeks of age, when he is careful to relieve himself away from his mother and littermates' nest. This desire to remain clean continues as the

house-train than puppies. Since healthy adult dogs have full control over their bladder and bowel movements, they are capable of "holding" for hours at a time and are less likely to make mistakes.

Knowing the signs. Whether you are training a puppy or an adult, it is important to recognize when your Boxer needs to relieve himself. Adults and puppies will need to eliminate immediately upon waking in the morning, within a half hour after eating, following periods of play or other physical activities, and at least once or more during the day. They also need to relieve themselves just before retiring for the night.

Young puppies (8 to 16 weeks) do not have as much control as older puppies or adult dogs, and will need to relieve themselves at additional times throughout the day. (Young male puppies may "dribble" across the floor when they are particularly excited. Young male and female puppies may urinate in a submissive gesture.) In other words, virtually *any time* is a potential time to urinate, and many times are opportunities to defecate. You can figure that a young puppy will need to relieve himself roughly every two to three hours throughout his waking and busy hours.

Fortunately, the Boxer puppy gains control fairly quickly. Bowel control comes first followed by bladder control. Around 14 weeks of age, the Boxer puppy usually already has control of his bowels, and is on the verge of controlling his bladder for longer periods of time. By 16 weeks of age, a puppy should be capable of sleeping comfortably through the night without any accidents.

puppy matures, so if you are careful to maintain and build on your Boxer's desire to be a clean dog, house-training should be a snap.

Older Boxers can be house-trained, too, with relatively few problems. Often, untrained adults are much faster to

Puppies and dogs alike often will seek out a place in the home that is hidden or away from view (and far away from what they consider their "nest") to relieve themselves. If you see your Boxer run behind a couch or go into another room, follow quickly! Take the pup outside and see if he has to relieve himself. As always, praise him when he relieves himself in the correct place.

Warning Signs

Before the Boxer puppy reaches the magical four-month stage of control and for many months thereafter, the owner must be particularly watchful. In addition to giving the puppy ample opportunities to urinate or defecate, the owner must learn to recognize the "I need to go" signs of a puppy and quickly take him outside to relieve himself.

For those who have not had a puppy in a long time, the signs of the puppy needing to urinate or defecate are the same as for an adult dog: He will halt his current activity and sniff the ground or circle the floor. With puppies, you've got to be quick! Their sequence of "preelimination" events can occur so rapidly that the owner has little or no time to prevent the puppy from relieving himself in the wrong place. Sometimes the puppy, similar to a busy toddler at play, may not even realize he has to "go" until it is too late to reach the appropriate location. For this reason, a very young puppy should be allowed only in areas of the home that have been floored with a surface that can be cleaned easily without any residual scent, such as

tile or vinyl. Avoid carpeted floors that are hard to clean and tend to retain odors.

The Basic Principle of Praise

Once you understand the limits of your Boxer and are better able to prevent accidents, the next basic concept of successful house-training is knowing when to praise, when to scold, and when not to do anything.

Rewarding the puppy or dog when he relieves himself outside or in a designated area is very important. The more times you can reward your Boxer for urinating

TRACY'S TIPS

Rare medical problems, such as UTIs or bladder stones, can hamper an owner's efforts to housetrain their Boxer. Be sure to check with your veterinarian to rule out medical issues if you are having difficulties housetraining your Boxer.

If your backyard has a patio or a deck, make sure you guide your puppy all the way to the grass to relieve himself. You want to make sure that he understands at an early age that the cement or brick patio or the wooden deck are not places he can eliminate.

or defecating outside, the faster he will learn that this is where you want him to go all the time.

However, when praising your Boxer for eliminating, don't get overly excited. This is the time for a gentle, soft-spoken, "Good dog. Good job," and a small treat immediately after he has chosen an appropriate place. If you let out loud praise while your Boxer is relieving himself, he is likely to stop what he is doing and come running to figure out what is so wonderful—and the concept of the praise for eliminating may be temporarily lost.

Timing. As for any scolding, gone is the old concept of dragging the dog or puppy to the site of an accident long after the actual act occurred and verbally or physically punishing the dog. Bad, bad, bad owner! This accomplishes nothing, except for worsening the situation: your Boxer will associate the scolding with the most recent event he has experienced, not the actual act of urinating or defecating.

For example, if you suddenly discover a wet spot on your carpet and call your Boxer over to the evidence on your carpet, and *then* scold him, what have you accomplished? Well, the last thing he remembers doing is coming when you called him. So, instead of piecing together that you are really angry about the wet spot, he thinks he's getting a tongue-lashing for coming when you called him. Now guess what? Instead of teaching him that relieving himself on the carpet is a "no-no," you've just taught him that he will be punished for coming when he is called.

So, what do you do when you discover that while you weren't looking, he relieved himself in the *wrong* place? Nothing. That's right. You do absolutely nothing. Simply take him outside, praise him gently but profusely when he relieves himself in the appropriate place, and then quietly clean up the accident.

The only time it is appropriate to say anything is *when you catch him in the act itself.* Say "ah-ah!" which should be just loud enough to get his attention and cause him to stop "midstream." If he is a young puppy, quickly pick him up without any anger and carry him outside. If he is an adult, quickly usher the dog outside.

Once the Boxer is outside, wait until he begins relieving himself. This may take a little while, since he is already upset and realizes that he has made you unhappy.

TRACY'S TIPS

I like to set my alarm for 4:30 A.M. with young puppies and require them to go out whether they are asking to or not. This helps with their success in keeping a dry bed. I do this from eight to twelve weeks of age.

Try to be calm and patient and forget for a minute what he just did. (Remember. It was an accident!) Once he settles down, he should quickly complete his duties. When this happens, praise him gently and reward him with a little treat.

Cleaning Up Mistakes

Since dogs tend to eliminate in areas in which they can find their scent, it is critical to eliminate any remnants of an accident in areas you do not want your Boxer to revisit. Unfortunately, his acute sense of smell will detect even minuscule amounts or urine or feces, so it is particularly important to clean up any accidents immediately and thoroughly.

The first rule of cleaning up mistakes is to remove as much of the offending matter as possible. For urine, blot up as much of the liquid as you can using paper towels. If your Boxer has defecated, pick up the stool carefully and remove all visible solid material.

Once all visible urine or feces is out of the way, use a pet stain and odor remover to neutralize the spot. There are specialized cleaners that use enzymes to break down the organic material in urine and stool, which can be very successful in removing all traces of smells. When cleaning urine spots in carpets, make sure you have used enough of the cleaning liquid to reach the urine that has soaked through to the carpet pad—and possibly even the subflooring. The amount of urine that was allowed to penetrate

the carpet's surface will dictate how much pet stain and odor remover you may have to use.

Pet Safe Cleaners

Finding cleaners that were effective in removing pet stains and smells often meant that dangerous residues could be left on the floor or carpet. (Dogs lick their paws, so toxic residues are particularly dangerous.) Now, it is possible to find safe and effective pet stain and odor removers. Many of the newer carpet and floor cleaners either use enzymes to break urine and/or microscopic fecal matter into harmless components, or contain antimicrobials that "eat" the pet urine or fecal remnants, leaving no toxic chemicals to clean up later.

Ammonia is very effective in killing germs; however, it happens to be one of the chemicals contained in dog's urine. When used in an attempt to clean a urine spot, the dog still smells ammonia, which could be confused with urine.

Try to avoid ammonia-based products for cleaning urine.

When using a pet stain and odor remover, follow directions carefully. If the product requires you to vacuum the area after a certain period of time, be sure to do so. This may be necessary to remove any potentially harmful residues. Also, always check the effects of the cleaner on a small area of the carpet or flooring (preferably where it can't be seen) to

check for color-fastness. There's nothing worse than having a bleached out area of carpet to mark the puppy's "spot."

The Importance of a Routine

In order to cut down on the potential number of accidents your Boxer may have over the course of his house-training, it is important to establish an eating and walking routine. The more regular and consistent you are with his feeding and walking schedule, the more likely he is to fall into a regular and predictable pattern of relieving himself.

As mentioned earlier in this chapter, both puppies and adults will need to relieve themselves shortly after eating meals. Knowing this, you can control this factor by providing your pet with meals scheduled at the same times every day (puppies three times a day, adults twice a day). A walk or an outside opportunity for him to defecate should be scheduled within a half hour after eating. Free-feeding, or allowing him to eat at will throughout the day, should be avoided since he will then need to defecate at various times throughout the day and perhaps even during the night.

Limiting Water

In order to control the frequency of urination, some house-training programs recommend limiting a puppy or dog's supply of water to the same periods in which he eats, and then picking up this water at other times throughout the day. This is *not* advisable. Fresh, cool water should not be withheld from your Boxer and should be available throughout the day, but water can be picked up after approximately two hours before his last opportunity to relieve itself at night. Limiting a dog's water supply to only a few times a day, however, may encourage gorging or drinking copious amounts of water in a short period of time, which is thought to be one of several reasons Boxers bloat. (Unless treated immediately by a veterinarian, bloat is often fatal.)

Putting It All Together

Two strategies that are commonly used to facilitate house-training include crate training or paper training. Depending on your long-term plans about how you'd like your dog to relieve himself, either method can work. Crate training is the preferred method for most dog owners and works well with Boxers of virtually all ages. Paper training is a method primarily reserved for young puppies.

Crate Training

The basic idea behind crate training is that the dog is kept in his crate whenever he cannot be watched closely by his owner. As noted earlier, because Boxers have a strong aversion to wetting or soiling their own area, they will refrain from relieving themselves as long as they can while they are in their crate.

A crate is a very safe way to transport a dog in the car. The use of a crate in the home can help reduce separation anxiety, prevent destructive behavior, and keep a curious Boxer from getting into dangerous household items.

With crate training, it is important that you always remember to crate the dog *only* after he has thoroughly relieved himself. To do otherwise would be setting him up for failure. Also, you need to realize that there is a limit to how many hours a Boxer can be crated at one stretch of time. Crating should be done *only* when you cannot watch him—not when you don't *feel* like watching him. There's a difference. The former makes for successful crate training, the latter for a physically and mentally unhealthy, cooped-up dog.

So, how long can you crate him? During the dog's active, day hours, he should never be crated beyond his physical limits to "hold." A good rule of thumb for figuring crate limits is to take his age in months, and add one hour up to a maximum range of seven or eight hours. For example, an eight-week-old puppy should not be crated for more than three hours at a time (two months plus one hour equals three hours). A six-month-old puppy, however, should be able to handle seven hours in a crate.

No dog should be confined for more than seven or eight hours during the day without the opportunity for a walk and some exercise. The Boxer's total crate time in a 24-hour period should not exceed 10 hours, if possible. This, of course, is difficult if the owner works long hours and no one is home. However, there are solutions to every situation (see Home Schooling, page 41).

During periods in which your Boxer is confined, make sure to provide him with a few safe toys—such as tough rubber balls that can be stuffed with treats or nylon bones—that will keep him happily occupied for periods of time. (Do not give him squeaky toys, rawhides, hooves, or bones from chicken or other meats that can be easily destroyed or bitten up into chunks. These chews could pose choking hazards.)

Of course, crate training works only if your Boxer enjoys sleeping and relaxing in his crate. Most Boxers readily accept crate confinement within a day or two if the crate is the proper size, is comfortably lined or padded, and if he is consistently rewarded with a treat and praised for entering the crate. The crate should never be used as punishment.

If your Boxer is not comfortable in a crate, see Habituating to the Crate, page 76.

Size. For a full-grown adult, the crate should be large enough for the dog to stand up, turn around, and lie down

---

Caution!

Boxers are notorious shredders of all things soft and swallowers of indigestible items, including shreds of towels, the fluff found in soft pillow beds, and hunks of fabric covers. Do not put towels, blankets, or soft bedding in the Boxer's crate when he's unattended until you absolutely know that he won't shred and eat his bedding. Ingesting bedding can be fatal and at a minimum will require surgery to remove a life-threatening blockage.

comfortably. Most Boxers will comfortably fit in a large crate, measuring roughly 24 inches wide × 36 inches deep × 26 inches high (61 × 91 × 66 cm). Smaller Boxers may fit a medium crate comfortably, and an exceptionally tall Boxer may require an extra-large size crate.

A puppy, of course, does not require an adult-size crate—at first. In fact, if the crate is to be used for house-training purposes, a much smaller crate is necessary. If you purchase an adult-size crate for a puppy, the puppy will have enough room in the crate to relieve himself in the corner and then lie safely away from the mess. Unfortunately, this sets your house-training efforts back a step because the puppy isn't taught to restrain her bowel or bladder movements.

With that said, you can do one of two things: First, you can purchase or borrow a smaller crate that fits the puppy for her first month or two, and then purchase a full-size crate when the puppy is five or six months old. Another option would be to buy a specially designed partition for your puppy's crate that makes a puppy-size crate out of an adult-size kennel. Whether you partition a larger crate or purchase or borrow a smaller crate, make sure the puppy's space is large enough for the puppy to stand, turn around, and lie down.

Crate types. Crates come in three styles: a hard shell, plastic crate; a wire, mesh style; and a soft, tentlike crate. All styles have their advantages, and whatever style you choose for your Boxer is mostly a matter of personal (and Boxer) preference.

1. The hard-shell plastic crate provides a more "denlike" feeling, but it has less

ventilation than a mesh-style crate, which shouldn't be a problem in the home but could be a problem if the crate is used in the back of a van or SUV with poor air circulation. The hard-shell kennel is the type that can be approved for air transportation should you ever need to ship your Boxer. These crates generally break down into two large pieces, so storing them takes up room. Also, cleaning up after an accident in this type of crate is generally easy; however, large messes will involve taking the crate apart and hosing it down in the backyard, in addition to scrubbing out every crack and fissure in the molded plastic.

2. The wire mesh crate is easy to break down and carry if it is a collapsible model. Cleaning out a mesh crate is simple, too, as the bottom pan slides out. Because the crate is mesh, the dog has a 360-degree view of his world and won't miss any action. Some dogs do not like the openness of the crate, while others may pull things in through the mesh, such as any blanket wrapping the crate. This crate is also not approved for airline travel.

3. The third type of crate is a tentlike crate that is constructed of plastic mesh and PVC tubing. The advantages to this type of crate are that it is feather light and folds down to the equivalent of a few hollow tubes. This may look like a good idea, but a Boxer can chew through the mesh panels in a matter of seconds and escape, or roll the crate over to the object of his desires and then chew it and/or escape. The tentlike crate is great if you are providing constant, light supervision; it is nothing short of disastrous for the unattended Boxer.

If you are adopting an adult Boxer, consult with the rescue about what type of crate the dog is used to and accepts. If your Boxer is used to a certain kind of crate, why mess with a good thing?

If you are purchasing or already own a Boxer puppy, he will most likely adapt to whatever style of crate you like the best. However, you might consider consulting your breeder for some input as to what type of crate his or her dogs seem to enjoy more.

Comfort. For bedding, be sure to use materials that are inexpensive and either washable, such as old towels or blankets, or disposable, such as shredded newspapers or pee pads. When he has mastered crate training, then you can consider more permanent bedding, such as specially made pads or fluffy dog beds.

Crate placement. Your Boxer's crate should be in the center of activity in your home. In this way, even when he is crated, he feels included in the household activities. The kitchen, breakfast room, or family room may be good locations in your home, depending on your lifestyle. At night, be sure to bring your Boxer—and his crate—to your bedroom.

Never banish the dog and crate to the basement or some other distant and lonely place. Boxers are true "people" dogs and separating them from people upsets them greatly, not to mention the fact that it takes a step back in their socialization process (see Socialization, pages 45–69). Also, make sure small children know the crate rules: No poking fingers or sticks into the crate; no banging toys on the roof or walls of the crate, and no sharing the crate. The crate is the Boxer's safe place and children should stay out.

Moving beyond the crate. When introducing your Boxer to larger spaces, it is wise to make this introduction in stages. For example, the first area to enlarge his privileges to might be an exercise pen in the kitchen with his crate in the pen. He might then be given full kitchen privileges. The floor in this room is usually an easy-to-clean surface, so if there is an accident, it can be cleaned up efficiently. Place the crate in the kitchen and then use dog gates or baby gates to block all exits to other rooms and hallways. After the puppy has thoroughly relieved himself outside, allow him a short period of play in the kitchen. If he gets excited, take him outside and allow him to relieve himself again. The goal here is to *avoid* an accident in the kitchen area and to praise continued successes outside. When you can't watch your puppy in the kitchen, crate him until you can.

Once he has proven he is trustworthy in the kitchen, with no mistakes for a week or more, and when he is at *least* four months old, you may want to introduce another room. Make sure your Boxer

is well walked and totally "empty" before introducing him to a new room. Again, watch him like a hawk. If he shows *any* signs of eliminating in this new room, take him outside immediately and encourage him to relieve himself.

Preventing *any* accidents and rewarding proper eliminations are the quickest way to succeed when expanding the dog's safe zones. Any mistake made during house-training is a step back and can leave a permanent scent marker for your dog. The more vigilant you are and the more opportunities you have to reward and praise the dog for good behaviors, the more success you will have with your dog.

Paper Training

Before crate training became popular, most owners taught their dogs to eliminate outside by what is referred to as paper training. This method has been used successfully by many dog owners, and if done properly, may be efficient for *some* Boxer owners.

Be forewarned, however, that when using the paper training method of house-training, there tends to be a greater margin of error—more "mistakes"—in the home before the dog masters the concept of going outside to relieve himself. The reason for this is that traditional paper training is really a two-step training process: First the puppy or dog must learn to eliminate *only* on the papered areas of a room. Then he must learn *not* to eliminate in the room, but only outside. It is often this transition from the first learning concept to the second that causes many dog owners trouble. Some dogs, after having learned that relieving themselves inside is acceptable, have difficulties understanding why they should relieve themselves outside.

Paper-trained dogs tend to search for paper surfaces in the house. Be forewarned that leaving the Sunday paper on the floor by the couch could be considered a proper place for a paper-trained Boxer to relieve himself.

To have a greater success rate with this house-training method, paper training should be used only as a "safety net" for the Boxer, not as an excuse to be less active in the dog's house-training. (It's easy to become lax when paper training a small puppy because the messes are small and can be picked up with the papers.) The same principles and level of effort to prevent accidents in crate training need to be applied to paper training.

Pee pads and Papering. To house-train a Boxer using the pee pad or paper training method, your first step is to choose a room that is suitable for this purpose. The kitchen usually works out well because it is centrally located—the puppy or adult never feels isolated—and the floor is generally of a material that is nonporous and cleans easily. Pee pads can be purchased in bulk and provide many added benefits for the added price—namely, they are absorbent and have a waterproof backing. Some also have small adhesive strips that keep the pads in place unlike newspapers, which can slide all over a slick floor.

1. Once you've selected the room, make sure you have all exits safely blocked using dog gates or baby gates to keep the Boxer in this room only. Then place a thick layer of newspapers over *the entire floor*. Little puppies can be paper-trained in a smaller area by using an exercise pen (x-pen). If a single x-pen is too small to contain the pup's crate and his play and eating area, consider purchasing a second x-pen to enlarge the area.

2. As with crate training, the dog should be fed, exercised, and allowed to relieve himself on a very regular schedule to avoid mishaps on the papered floor. Even though there are papers on the floor to catch accidents, you should not become lazy or inattentive to your puppy's needs. If he shows signs of needing to relieve himself, rush him outside with the command "*Outside*," and praise him profusely when he relieves himself. Praise and reward every outside success.

3. As the puppy grows older, remove more and more pee pads or papers from the floor until only one corner of the room still contains pads or papers. If the Boxer has been using the papers to relieve himself, he will generally seek out these papers no matter where they are placed.

4. When you have worked your way down to a single, small area of the room that is papered or has one remaining pee pad, and your Boxer is old enough that he can be expected to "hold" for however many hours you are gone at a time, take the final pad or paper outside, with some scent remaining on it, and place it in the grass with the Boxer watching. He should then be allowed to sniff this new placement of the papers and encouraged to eliminate. Pick up and throw away the papers.

5. Be sure to leave an area outside in the grass with a bit of scent to help your dog connect that the backyard is where he should be going. Continue to praise him every time he relieves himself in the appropriate place.

Bell Training

Some Boxers are very vocal and animated when expressing their need to relieve themselves. Other Boxers are more of the "silent type." To ensure that you know when your house-trained Boxer needs to go outside, hang a set of sleigh bells over the doorknob leading to the backyard. Make sure the bells hang low enough so that if you have a puppy, he can ring the bells with his nose or hit them with his paws.

Each time you go to open the door to let your Boxer outside to relieve himself, encourage him to touch the bells with his nose or paw. Simply touching the bells with your finger can be enough to entice him to touch the bells. If he needs a little more encouragement, use a treat to lure him closer to the bells, treating him for his progress until he eventually rings the bells. Praise and treat him for ringing the bells—and then let him outside.

It won't take long before your Boxer will ring the bells so that he can be let outside.

Dog Doors

One way to facilitate the learning processes involved in paper training is to consider installing a dog door from the kitchen, or whatever room you are using for house training, to the backyard. The dog door allows the dog to go outside to relieve himself whenever he needs to, whether or not you are home. In the early stages, you will need to continue to praise and reward him for going outside to relieve himself; however, within a relatively short period of time, he will jump through the door whenever he needs to.

If you are considering installing a dog door, keep in mind that the indoor portion of your home still needs to be an area of confinement for the dog. The indoor area should not be too large; just because the Boxer can go outside anytime to relieve himself doesn't mean he *will*. If you have other adult dogs in the home, however, you will be amazed at how quickly your puppy follows the adult dogs' lead and learns to hop through the door to relieve himself outside.

The confinement area needs to be small enough that the Boxer considers it "home." It also needs to be an area that is easily cleaned. (Keep in mind that whatever room the dog door leads to will see a lot of traffic, including muddy Boxer paws, unearthed chew toys, and other such debris and dirt.) The dog door is not an instant house-training fix, but it does facilitate learning in many cases.

If you install a dog door and you are gone (leaving your Boxer unattended), make sure your yard is absolutely Boxer-proof and your Boxer cannot scale or dig under your fence. It may be necessary to place the dog door in a secure, shaded kennel run within your yard to give your Boxer the freedom to go outside to relieve himself while making sure he doesn't have the opportunity to escape.

Overcoming Lifestyle Complications

In a perfect puppy world, a Boxer owner would live at home and would attend to the puppy's needs day and night. If this were the case, house-training would be completed in short order and the whole process would theoretically involve no accidents.

This isn't a perfect world, of course. With dual-income families, many times the Boxer puppy or adult is left alone during the day and supervision can be given only in the evenings and at night. Other Boxer owners live in apartments or condominiums with no backyard. Both situations are manageable; they just take a bit more effort from the owner.

Latchkey Boxers. For the Boxer that is left alone most of the day, you will need to create a situation in which he can use a dog door to a confined, safe area or a fenced backyard, or make arrangements to have him attended to periodically through the day.

If you have an adult dog you are trying to house-train, a midday break should be sufficient. If you can dash home on your lunch hour, or hire a pet walker to walk him, the adult dog should be happy until you can rejoin him in the evening.

If you have a puppy, you will need to make more visits home, or hire someone to do this for you. If you walk, feed, and then walk your puppy again before you leave for work at 7:00 A.M., your puppy will need relief by 9:00 or 10:00 A.M. He

will then need to be fed again at noon, and walked. Three o'clock would be the next break for this little fellow and then again at 6:00 P.M. when you walk through the door and before you feed the puppy supper. Additional walks at 8:00 P.M. and 10:00 P.M. would be advisable to make sure the puppy is completely empty before curling up for the night.

Older puppies (6 months and up) should manage with one or two relief visits during the day.

Apartment dwellers. If you rent an apartment or live in a condominium, you very likely do not have a backyard and must rely on walking your Boxer to allow him to relieve himself. If this is the case, leash-training him immediately is particularly important (see Walk Nicely, page 108). It is also important that your Boxer can differentiate between a nice, long walk and the "relief" walk in which you want him to go right now, right here.

For this, you'll need to train him with the potty command (see page 36).

City dawg. Some Boxer owners do not have the convenience of having a patch of grass for their dogs' use and must "curb" their dogs. Though this sounds difficult, it just takes practice. Many urban dogs can be taught to "curb" if this is the only area in which they have an option of relieving themselves.

When walking your Boxer, watch for signs that he may need to relieve himself. Move him quickly to the street side of the curb. While he is relieving himself, be sure to give him the potty command and then praise him gently. With some repetition, your Boxer will be able to "curb" quite well.

Note: Picking up after your dog is very important. When taking walks be sure to carry "potty" bags, sold in pet stores everywhere. Seal and throw away in an appropriate receptacle.

40

Home Schooling

Common House-training Problems

Problem. Whenever I let my Boxer puppy into the family room, he runs to the same spot behind the couch and urinates. What should I do?

Solutions. This common problem usually occurs when an owner trusts the Boxer a little too soon with a little too much. First, the owner should thoroughly clean the area to which the puppy is running. This spot is attractive to the dog because it has a lingering scent. If the scent is into the carpet pad—or even the subflooring—this will need to be treated to remove the scent. Second, the owner should "block" this spot, which may be as simple as dragging the couch over the area that the puppy likes to use. Dogs also do not like to relieve themselves near their food, so feeding the puppy in this area may also be an option. Third, the owner should restrict the puppy from this room *unless two things have occurred*: 1) the puppy has totally relieved himself immediately before entering the room, and 2) the owner can provide the puppy with his or her undivided attention and watch for "warning" signs of the puppy's need to relieve himself.

Problem. My Boxer was house-trained, but now he is urinating in his crate.

Solutions. Have you changed any part of your routine recently? Sometimes owners "forget" the needs of their well-trained Boxers and start to become lax in their feeding, walking, and exercising schedule, or simply begin asking too much from their Boxers. If his routine has not been changed and he is suddenly urinating in his crate or elsewhere in the home, schedule an appointment with your veterinarian. There are many diseases that can cause excessive urination.

Problem. My male Boxer is marking my living room couch.

Solutions. If an adolescent or adult male is marking one particular piece of furniture, make it inaccessible to the dog—*unless you are present and watching*. Catching the dog in the act may put an end to this action. Also, make sure to thoroughly clean the furniture to remove all traces of the dog's scent.

If these actions fail, and if your Boxer is not neutered, you may want to consider having him altered. Researchers report that up to 60 percent of males with territorial problems stop this behavior when they are altered. Serious cases of marking may require other interventions, such as wearing a pee band. In severe cases of marking—and when neutering has not altered the behavior—certain medications that have been approved for lessening territorial behaviors might be appropriate and may be recommended by your veterinarian.

Problem. My Boxer won't alert me when he has to go outside, he just finds a spot in another room.

Solutions. Thoroughly clean all "accidents" in the home and start over with the Boxer's house-training. A dog that does not signal an owner that he needs to go outside has not learned the basics of house-training. The use of a crate will facilitate the "alerting" portion of this training; the Boxer will not want to soil his area and will typically bark or cry when he needs to relieve himself. Once trained to alert you when in a crate, his house-training gradually can be broadened to include a room at a time—under your watchful eye. When you can't keep a close eye on the dog or if you are involved in another task, he should be returned to his crate, or kept on a leash tied to your belt. The leash will prevent any "dashing off" by the Boxer and will help him to alert his owner to any outside needs.

Problem. My wife and I are gone all day. How can we possibly house-train our Boxer?

Solutions. Until the Boxer reaches seven or eight months of age—when he can "hold" for seven or eight hours at a time—working owners need to be a little creative and come up with daytime solutions for their Boxers-in-training. One solution is to take a lunch break at home. This will provide him with roughly half an hour of exercise, attention, and an opportunity to relieve himself.

If you live too far away for this to be feasible, consider having a trusted neighbor, relative, or retiree help with Boxer duties during the day. If you have a fenced backyard, the duties will be as simple as letting the dog out for half an hour, a little bit of play, and then re-kenneling the dog. Pet sitters are also available in many areas of the country, and can be hired for these same services.

If you have a backyard and a "safe" room leading to this backyard, you may want to consider a dog door to this area (see Dog Doors, page 38). Dog doors are a terrific way to allow your Boxer free access to the outdoors without subjecting them to severe summer or winter temperatures.

Problem. My elderly Boxer has started to urinate on himself when he sleeps. What can I do?

Solutions. Incontinence generally occurs in overweight, older, spayed female dogs; however, incontinence can occur in males, too. To rule out possible illnesses that could also cause leakage, the Boxer should first be examined by a veterinarian. When conditions and/or diseases are ruled out and incontinence is determined to be the issue, there are many things you can do to help your Boxer:

- Keep him light. Excessive fat can add pressure to the bladder and cause more leakage. If your Boxer is overweight, help him trim up by reducing calories carefully and increasing his daily exercise.
- Exercise. In addition to helping with achieving a healthy weight, exercise will also help to tone and tighten muscles that can lessen pressure on the dog's bladder.
- Monitor water intake. Allow unlimited cool water access to your Boxer during the day. About an hour before the Boxer's bedtime, offer him a final drink and then pick up his water bowl. Allow him to fully relieve himself before going to bed for the night.
- Limit access. Keep the incontinent Boxer in an area of the home that is easily cleaned, such as the kitchen. Use a baby or dog gates to keep him in this area with waterproof bedding (see below).
- Waterproof bedding. Protect floors, furniture, and dog beds by placing a rubberized pad (such as those sold to protect baby cribs) or pee pads under your Boxer's favorite places to lie. Tuck these under soft blankets to protect beds and furniture, and in between the cover of his dog bed and the soft padding.
- Wash frequently. Clean soaked bedding, blankets, and other surfaces as soon as a leak is noted. Gently clean your Boxer after every leak so that his skin doesn't suffer from urine burn.
- Medications can help. Several oral medications can be prescribed when other methods (weight loss and exercise) have failed to help. These medications are prescription only. They are inexpensive, easy to dose (chewables are available for some medications), and have very few side effects (if any).
- Surgery. For female Boxers that haven't responded to medication, surgery may be recommended to alleviate the dog's incontinence. A surgery that has shown success in alleviating incontinence in dogs involves injecting collagen into the urethra.

TRACY'S TIPS

A great resource for owners of incontinent Boxers is www. handicappets.com. This site offers elevated mesh pet crate floors, waterproof pet bedding, and other helpful items.

5 *Socialization*

Is a good-natured, happy, well-adjusted Boxer the result of nature or nurture? It's much like the chicken and the egg question in that no one has a definitive answer but *everyone* has an opinion! So what's the right answer?

Opinions aside, and avoiding the chicken and egg question entirely, a dog's temperament and resulting behaviors are the result of both nature, through genetics, and nurture, through life experiences. Where the water gets muddied is in determining specifically *how much* influence genetics and environment have on the final outcome of a dog's temperament.

It is commonly accepted that a puppy is not born with an entirely "clean slate." Long before the puppy is whelped, she is genetically predisposed to have certain characteristics. Whether she reaches her full genetic potential is, however, dependent on her environment—how she is raised, nurtured, and shaped. Some experts estimate that a puppy's environment, or nurturing, influences up to 40 percent of the dog's adult temperament.

So in theory, a puppy that is predisposed to be timid or fearful *could* be raised in an enriched, friendly environment that would suppress this genetic tendency. Conversely, it could be possible that a puppy that is predisposed to be friendly and outgoing could become fearful if she is exposed to a severe environment as a puppy.

This is why the genetics of temperament and the influences of learning environments are so important to the Boxer owner. It explains why, even if a Boxer puppy comes from parents with extremely nice temperaments, it is not a guarantee that the puppy will develop into a model Boxer. The "environment" and life experiences you provide your Boxer will, however, go far in ensuring that your puppy becomes a "social" animal.

In the Beginning . . .

Some research indicates that the shaping of your Boxer's temperament may begin before she is actually born. Recent studies indicate that factors such as the position of the puppy in the mother's uterus and the mother's physical and mental state can affect the puppy's behavioral development.

Soon after birth, the puppy goes through an important phase of development with her mother and littermates. During this time, many of the puppy's "dog" behaviors are learned. It is also a time during which the puppy develops much of her trust of humans. For this reason, it is critical that puppies are handled gently and given a lot of human attention from birth. To raise them away from humans (i.e., in the backyard or in a kennel) is to deprive them of this contact,

TRACY'S TIPS

It can't be stressed enough how important it is to never separate a puppy from her littermates and mother before the age of eight weeks. Puppies that are sold at early ages often suffer from a host of problems later on, including fear aggression, dog–dog aggression, and possibly a lack of bite inhibition.

which is thought to result in the potential development of serious behavioral problems as the puppy matures.

Young puppies also learn how to filter sounds of a home from their mom. A well-adjusted, social Boxer mom won't react fearfully or aggressively to typical noises, such as a door shutting, the toilet flushing, or children laughing loudly—so her puppies grow up accepting these sounds as commonplace, too. A fearful or aggressive Boxer mom, however, will mold her puppies' responses after her own So, if she responds inappropriately (with fear or aggression) toward certain sounds or people, the pups will learn to respond in the same manner to these noises, things, and people.

Socialization with People

Once your puppy is home, she is in a critical socialization period. For about a month, or until the age of roughly 12 weeks, the experiences that your puppy lives through greatly infuences how your puppy develops mentally and emotionally. One of your responsibilities during this time—and for the months following—is to socialize your Boxer with people. No matter how happy and sociable a puppy is, if she is kept in virtual isolation alone with her owner, there is a strong possibility that as an adult dog she will not respond appropriately with strangers either in the home or out and about in public.

With the legal liabilities that are present today, not working with your Boxer to ensure she is friendly with all types of people is a serious mistake. Fortunately, Boxers are by nature a gregarious sort and have an affinity toward loving all people, but don't take for granted that this nature will fully develop without your help. Remember, it takes a combination of good genetics *and* a positive upbringing to develop a well-balanced, friendly, social Boxer.

It Takes All Kinds

The key to successful socialization training is to introduce your Boxer to lots of different people. It's important to ensure that every exposure to people is a positive one.

Children. Kids are typically drawn to puppies like magnets, so if you live in a neighborhood with children, just taking a walk every day will provide the exposure your puppy needs to this group. Lots of pats from children of all ages are just what your Boxer needs to reaffirm her natural love of little humans. If you don't live in a neighborhood with children, consider taking her to a park that is frequented by children. Or invite a friend with children over from time to time for some supervised play with her.

Neighbors. Introducing your Boxer to your neighbors in a controlled and pleasant manner has a twofold benefit. One is that she will be able to meet more types of people, and two is that your neighbors will see how affable she is. At best, they will love your dog, too; at worst, they will at least understand that she is not dangerous and that you are a responsible owner.

People in uniform. The importance of teaching your Boxer to respect and like people in uniform lies in the fact that if she *doesn't* like these folks, you're likely to have your mail held and your packages go undelivered. And for good reason. The statistics of postal workers being bitten

by dogs along their routes is staggering. So, be sure to do your part and introduce your Boxer at an early age to every delivery person who comes on a regular or even frequent basis. Your delivery person will greatly appreciate your efforts.

Hint: Never allow your Boxer unsupervised access to the front door. If she is allowed to bark at delivery people when they come to the door, she will think that her barking has successfully driven the person away. This activity is self-rewarding for the Boxer in that she thinks that her barking forced the delivery person to turn around and leave. It worked! Unfortunately, the successful "driving off" of a stranger from the door rewards territorial behavior. If you can't supervise your Boxer at the front door, keep her gated away from view.

TRACY'S TIPS

Including environmental enrichment at a young age is very important for your Boxer, so don't just walk her around the same neighborhood everyday—take her places. Parks will have lots of new smells. Take her to an outdoor shopping mall and walk the sidewalks, meeting people with packages, observing rolling carts, and comfortable traffic. Go explore a local bike trail. Take your puppy to a kids' park. Make it fun, fun, fun for your Boxer!

Rules of Engagement

When socializing your Boxer with people, it's not the quantity of interactions that is important but rather the quality. Whether you're socializing a puppy or an adult dog, there are three basic rules to follow.

1. **Keep It Positive**. Meetings with people should be happy, fun experiences. The only way for a Boxer to learn that people of all sizes, shapes, colors, and ages are *good* is for her to meet good, friendly, dog-loving people in a positive, rewarding, and relaxed manner.

   A positive meeting is one in which your Boxer is relaxed and happy to meet the stranger and is without any trepidation. In order to ensure this, you will need to be keenly aware of your Boxer's body language and watch for any signs of stress or mixed signals (See Home Schooling: Body Language Primer for guidelines, page 49.)

   When your Boxer meets someone new and the meeting is friendly and outgoing, reward her! Do this with gentle voice praise (*"What a good girl!"*) You can also reward her with treats (have the stranger offer a tidbit) but generally most Boxers adore attention so much that the pats and love from a new person is a huge reward in itself for the dog.

2. **Quality vs. Quantity**. Though it would be wonderful for a gregarious Boxer to positively meet 100 new people in her first month with her new owner, the number of meetings is far less important than the quality of the meetings One poor meeting (for example, a meeting in which the puppy or adult is frightened by the stranger) can undo *weeks* worth of socialization and, depending on how badly the meeting went, the Boxer could have a permanent fear of this particular individual or an aspect of the individual (i.e., a ball cap, sunglasses, people in puffy coats, etc.) So, it is far better to have twenty great meetings with people than try to push your Boxer and have her experience a "mixed bag" of meetings.

3. **Follow Your Boxer's Lead**. This is perhaps the most important rule of all when socializing a Boxer of any age: Never force your Boxer to meet *anyone.* If your Boxer eagerly wants to meet a person, let her! If she is hesitant or shows any sign of stress, fear, or mixed signals (friendliness and fear at the same time, for example), immediately give your Boxer more *space* or distance from the person. Wait for your Boxer to decide to meet the person, and then let her move toward the person on her own. Reward!

Body Language Primer

Understanding when your Boxer is comfortable and relaxed versus stressed or anxious can go far in helping to keep socialization with both people and other dogs positive experiences. The key is to keep the Boxer from ever showing signs of stress, anxiety, fear, or aggression. Knowing your Boxer's stress signs is also critical to keeping training sessions positive and productive. A stressed Boxer is a confused Boxer—and a sign that you need to change gears. Make it fun and simpler for your Boxer before building up a particular exercise or skill.

So, whether socializing with dogs or people, in a training session or even just out and about, it is important to understand not only when your Boxer is becoming stressed, but also what action to take to make your Boxer more comfortable and relaxed again.

Friendly, Relaxed Body Language

The at-ease Boxer is easy to recognize. Her head carriage is comfortable, between 60 and 80 degrees, and her head wrinkles are natural, giving the overall expression of friendliness and/or mild curiosity. Head cocking is a classic curious Boxer move, and endearing in itself. The relaxed Boxer's eyes are expressive, warm, and round, with her eyebrows expressing inquisitiveness. If a Boxer has cropped ears, they are not fully upright when relaxed unless

she is listening to something with mild interest. The natural-eared Boxer may prick her ears to listen or if she is interested in something; however, the body remains relaxed. Boxers that are comfortable in their surroundings frequently pant in an easy manner, giving a wide-mouthed, happy smile appearance.

The relaxed Boxer's body is loose, unless she is particularly happy to see someone, and then she can be overcome with a full-body wriggle that epitomizes pure Boxer joy and love. Her docked tail is relaxed and generally carried low or level to her back. Wagging is loose and regular, with a happy dog wagging furiously but with

a lower tail carriage that creates a full-body wriggle. If a Boxer has a natural tail, the relaxed Boxer will have a big, loose tail wag, with the rate of wag increasing with her happy excitement, but it remains level or low.

Vocally, the happy, content Boxer ranges from being absolutely silent to a range of "talking" sounds. If she is barking, it is a distinctive happy bark.

Watching for Transitions

If your Boxer is showing friendly, relaxed body language, all is good with the world. If you see your Boxer fade these behaviors or stand still without exhibiting any discernable happy behaviors, your Boxer is in transition.

This is the moment you either need to move your Boxer farther away from what has captured her interest or remove her completely from a forming situation. If you can prevent your Boxer from becoming stressed or, worse yet, from becoming frightened or aggressive, you have won more than half the battle. Identify the source of your Boxer's concern, and you can work toward making her more comfortable with the situation from a safer distance.

The Stressed Boxer

The Boxer that is becoming stressed or anxious may slightly tighten her neck, and you may see her turn her head away or avoid eye contact with what-

ever is stressing her. A severely stressed Boxer's pupils will be dilated and she may exhibit abnormal blinking. Her eyelids may also tighten slightly, giving her a nervous expression.

The Boxer with cropped ears may noticeably shift her ears in a more forward and alert position, or conversely shift them backwards. The natural-eared Boxer's ears will also either rock backward or slightly forward. Often, a stressed Boxer (of both ear types) will shift between positions of stress and comfort.

The stressed Boxer, if she was panting, will often *stop* panting and suddenly shut her mouth. If her mouth was closed (i.e., it is cool outside and she wasn't excited), she may begin panting nervously (a higher rate than normal). The stressed Boxer may drool or exhibit lip smacking. The most common Boxer sign of stress, however, is the yawn.

The tail of the stressed Boxer is usually marked with mixed signals. The tail may cease wagging, shift from friendly wagging to no wagging to fearful wagging to a stiffer aggressive position, back to friendliness or stillness.

The Boxer may also exhibit some classic stress behaviors, such as giving a full-bodied shake, as if the dog was wet (but isn't) or is trying to shake off the stress. Other signs of stress include stretching (but the Boxer isn't tired) and scratching (but there's no itch). A young puppy may suddenly scramble to her owner and scratch or claw to get up into your arms.

Fearful Body Signs

Just as the happy, exuberant Boxer is easy to spot, so is the fearful Boxer. When frightened or intimidated by something, the Boxer will physically lower her body so that she appears to be cringing. Even her tail will lower or even completely tuck tightly against her rear end. (Note: the fearful Boxer may very well continue to wag her tail but it will wag in a tucked position). She may also show piloerection, with the hair from her neck to the base of her tail raised, or urinate submissively. Other fearful behaviors include a tight and trembling body, or flopping over onto the back to expose the belly.

The frightened Boxer will lower her head and look upward or sideways without moving her head, presenting a "half-moon" eye look that exposes the whites of her eyes. Her eyelids will often tighten, giving a nervous expression, and she will try to avert her eyes and avoid direct eye contact. The natural-eared Boxer's ears will rock backward, but the crop-eared Boxer's positioning is perhaps most dramatic, as the normally erect ears will literally appear to pin against the dog's neck.

The fearful Boxer will increase her rate of panting; her lips will draw back in a nervous, tightened position—but her teeth are not exposed in an aggressive manner. She may remain silent, or

ner. Her eyes will be hard, with a direct stare, and pupils may be dilated. Her eyes may narrow but this tightening of lids is distinctly different in appearance from a nervous, stressed tightening. Ears, whether cropped or natural, will be fully forward in a hard, focused manner.

The aggressive Boxer's body will be ramrod stiff and every muscle flexed as the dog appears to be standing on her toes and straining forward, or she may be lunging on the leash with intent to harm. She may or may not have pilo-erection. Her docked (or natural) tail will be carried as high as possible and exceptionally stiff looking at the base. *She may be wagging her tail*, but look for the distinctive stiffness and slower or erratic wagging pattern.

The highly agitated Boxer may growl, snarl, or bark in a menacing manner (this bark is distinct from a friendly bark or even an alert bark). Additionally, the Boxer may be silent *with her mouth closed*, which can be a sign that the Boxer is about to bite.

If you see your Boxer exhibiting aggressive behaviors, you may have less than a split-second to react to prevent a disastrous situation. It is far easier to prevent aggressive behavior from occurring by watching your dog's body language and keeping an eye out for transitional behavior—the subtle shift from friendly, relaxed behavior to one of stress, which if not addressed, can lead to fear or aggression.

she could whimper, whine, or cry. Alternatively, a fearful Boxer may also begin barking in a last ditch attempt to make the object of her fear back away.

Aggressive Behaviors

Aggression in Boxers can occur for a myriad of reasons—from fear (when the Boxer feels she has no recourse but to "fight"), to territory (defending a place, such as a backyard), to dominance (asserting a position with other dogs or people in a physical way). According to some behaviorists, there are more than 30 forms of and reasons for aggression in dogs.

Aggressive behaviors are easily recognizable in the Boxer. The overall appearance of the Boxer's look is threatening and intense. Her neck will become stiff and taut, with a high, stiff head carriage—or she may drop her head slightly in a menacing, stiff man-

The Shy Boxer

Working with the Timid Boxer

The majority of dog bites are believed to stem from fear biting—not aggression, as most people might think. So, why would a fearful dog bite? Wouldn't she rather run away than bite? The answer is yes, the fearful dog *would* prefer to avoid conflict; however, if the fearful dog senses that she *can't* run away, her heightened fear will cause her to react with an aggressive response to drive the source of her fear away. For example, a dog chained in a yard cannot physically run away from someone who comes into the yard. The chained dog knows she cannot escape so her only resort (to avoid having the scary person touch her) is to drive the person away. If ferocious barking and snapping don't do it, maybe a bite will.

A fearful puppy or dog on a leash is not dissimilar to the dog on a chain When meeting new people, the Boxer can only get as far away as the length of the leash. If a fearful Boxer is forced to meet someone she is afraid of, at a minimum it will not be a positive experience. The worst-case scenario is that the Boxer growls, barks, lunges, snaps, or bites.

This situation can be completely avoided if the owner is observant (watching for the subtle changes in his or her dog's body language) and is willing to work with the timid dog to increase her confidence and comfort level around people. In addition to following the basic guidelines of meet and greets with

Many people, when their puppies are trying to avoid meeting someone, will push or pull the dog forward and try to "talk" the Boxer into meeting the stranger. Dogs cannot be verbally reasoned with in the same way as small children who may be leery of meeting someone. Your Boxer will not understand, "Oh, don't worry about Mr. Jones. He's a nice man!" All your Boxer will know is that she is being dragged toward the scariest person she's ever seen, and she wants nothing more than to get away from this man. Forcing your Boxer to meet someone will heighten her fear and will create a very negative encounter.

people (most importantly, follow the rule of allowing the Boxer to make the approach), the following are some additional guidelines when working with a timid Boxer.

1. **Understanding your Boxer's body language.** A fear bite almost always is preceded by distinct behaviors and/or changes in behaviors. It does not come out of nowhere! If you understand your Boxer's behaviors and clearly know what constitutes friendly, relaxed body language versus *transitioning* (the lack of friendly, relaxed body language) you can prevent your timid Boxer from becoming stressed in the first place

2. **Know what stresses your Boxer.** For some puppies, it might be people who are tall. For others, it might be people wearing ball caps or sunglasses. An adult dog with limited socialization may be more leery of men. If you *know* what your Boxer is sensitive to, you are better equipped to help your puppy or adult overcome her fear, or at least be more comfortable.

3. **Watch for the moment of transition.** A few seconds before a Boxer

will become fearful, stressed, or anxious with a stranger, she will *transition* from a happy, loose-bodied, relaxed pup to a Boxer devoid of friendly behaviors. She won't be showing signs of stress or anxiety, but she definitely won't be showing friendly behaviors. At this point, you have but a few seconds to do something to keep the meeting positive—and your best move is to *move away*.

4. **Give your Boxer more space *immediately*.** Remember the dog on the chain that can't move away and feels she is forced to fight? This is the decision your Boxer is making when she transitions. She is uneasy and is trying to figure out what to do—fight or flight (or any number of generations of actions between the two). Help her by offering her more space and more time to figure out that the stranger is okay. Keep moving her away from the stranger until she is again relaxed and happy. This could be a few feet, a few yards, or across the street

5. **Allow friendly meetings, according to your Boxer's cues.** If you've moved your Boxer away from someone and your Boxer relaxes and then shows interest in meeting someone, allow her to approach the person

6. **Help the particularly timid Boxer.** Many people who would like to meet your Boxer may not realize that they are behaving in what your Boxer might see as aggressive behaviors. If you have a very shy Boxer, try to introduce your Boxer to people who are dog-savvy and instinctively know how to let a shy puppy or dog approach them, such as

the staff at your veterinarian's office, dog trainers at your obedience club, fellow owner/trainers at an agility center, etc.

Additionally, if you feel comfortable working with people (this involves a little bit of confidence), you can coach strangers on how to greet your Boxer. The rules should include:

a) Allow the Boxer to make her own approach.
b) Make no direct eye contact.
c) Do not bend over the dog or pup.
d) Do not pet the dog on the top of the head—instead, extend a palm up hand and scratch the dog under her chin.
e) Ignore the Boxer until she is comfortable and showing friendly behaviors.
f) Move very slowly and speak softly.
g) Offer a treat when the owner (you) says the dog is showing positive behaviors.

7. Be your timid Boxer's advocate.

So often owners of shy, fearful, or timid dogs are embarrassed. They want to show off their beautiful Boxer and they want her to love everyone. Forcing a Boxer to meet someone that she's afraid of, however, will have a negative effect on her socialization. Be patient. Don't isolate your Boxer from people but continue to offer quality meetings with people you know or dog people who understand what you're trying to achieve. Every positive encounter adds up in the overall scheme of experiences and provides your Boxer with one more reason to meet the next person!

8. Engage your Boxer in confidence-building activities.

Many a shy dog has gained confidence in sports such as agility and has also been able to develop better people social skills when around experienced, doggie-friendly handlers. Obedience is also a terrific way to work on ways to distract your Boxer when working around people, and it can indirectly help her to become more comfortable when working in proximity of people.

Additionally, make sure the "stranger" avoids direct eye contact with her, which she may take as a direct threat. Then have the person toss a tidbit to your dog. Praise her! As she becomes less fearful and more trusting of new people, you can decrease the distance at which the person is tossing the food, until the individual is close enough to feed the tidbit by hand.

If someone comes into your home, allow the Boxer to approach the person on her own terms. Have your friend sit in a chair or on the floor, with his or her head turned slightly away from the dog and avoiding eye contact. Yawning once or twice can also help to calm a nervous dog. When the dog looks to be a little curious, have the friend gently (no big motions) toss the treat in the direction of the dog. Gradually let the Boxer come to the person.

Don't rush socializing a shy Boxer or push her too fast. It may take days, weeks, or even months of work for a very frightened Boxer to really begin to trust all humans. However, if you keep up this exercise and don't push her "comfort zone" too much each time, you will

common problem than timidness—and it is the better of the two behavior "problems" to have. Exuberance, however, needs to be reined in without squashing the Boxer's natural love for people.

The act of jumping up on people is a friendly dog behavior. What you don't want to do is to pull back sharply on your Boxer or yell at her "*No!*" when she flings herself at someone in a boisterous Boxer greeting. If you "correct" her for what she sees as a friendly greeting, she won't link that it's the jumping up behavior that you don't like, but rather that being friendly with strangers is what she shouldn't do. What a conundrum!

To get around this problem, you need to be able to control your Boxer's enthusiasm in a positive way. Teach her the *sit* (see page 99). When she is in a *sit*, then the stranger can pet her. You will find that once your gregarious Boxer associates the *sit* with pats and attention, she will often skid into a wriggly *sit* just to receive pats from strangers—with no command from you!

Note: Only put your Boxer in a *sit* if she is an overly exuberant greeter. Putting a fearful or timid Boxer in a *sit* to prevent her from backing away from a stranger will heighten her fear and worsen the situation. See page 53 for advice on dealing with timid Boxers.

begin to see gradual and even immediate improvement.

Also, be careful not to reward bad behavior either directly (with a treat) or indirectly by giving the dog verbal reassurances. As mentioned earlier, rewarding the dog in any way when she acts frightened or growls will inadvertently reward her for her poor behavior.

Hint: Since you are using treats as the reward in this exercise, your Boxer may be more amenable to strangers with food if this exercise is done *before* the puppy or adult has had a meal and is just a bit on the hungry side . . .

The Exuberant Boxer

Jumping up on strangers and slathering them with Boxer kisses generally is a more

What Is a Negative Experience?

Anytime the Boxer is forced to greet someone and her body language is not relaxed, she shows signs of stress, fear, or even aggression. Less obvious but also negative experiences include those in which the Boxer shows mixed signals, such as a happy tail wag that becomes lowered (a fearful tail wag), and the puppy rolls over or urinates in submission. Another mixed signal greeting would be a rapid, lowered tail wag with a crouching approach (fearful), mixed with barking.

It is best to avoid a negative experience completely by following the advice in Rules of Engagement (see page 48) and Working with the Timid Boxer (see page 53), which is good to know even if your Boxer isn't timid. Of course, we're human and there will be a time when a meeting is not entirely positive. Usually, this will occur when you're distracted with something else and not watching your Boxer closely. It happens.

When this happens, back out of the situation calmly and give your Boxer space between her and the stranger. Allow her to relax and greet the stranger on *her* terms—and only if she is eager, relaxed, and happy. Sometimes it just takes a Boxer a moment to figure out a situation. Don't fret and don't "correct" the Boxer for timid behavior; it will only increase her fear of strangers.

Also, if your Boxer has a negative experience, don't mistakenly reward or praise her stressful or fearful behavior. It's human nature to comfort someone who is afraid or nervous, but this doesn't help a fearful or stressed dog. It actually does the opposite—coddling a dog either verbally or physically confirms to the dog that she was correct for being fearful. You have rewarded her. Instead, be calm and have

the air of an "I have you covered" sense of confidence as you move her away from the source of her stress. Reward her only when she has been showing calm, relaxed body language for at least three seconds without any mixed signals.

Adopted Adults and People Socialization

If you've adopted an adult Boxer from a breed rescue or shelter, and she has been temperament-tested sufficiently, the people there will know your dog's likes and dislikes, as well as her level of socialization. If she is very friendly with people, keep up the good work! Continue to reinforce these good behaviors.

However, if your Boxer is fearful of people—or of specific groups of people, such as children, people with baseball caps, men, etc.—make sure to work on this in a positive way (see The Shy Boxer, page 53). Many adopted Boxers simply need time and patience before they begin to trust humans again. Be sure to give them this adjustment period.

Socializing Your Boxer with Other Dogs

Though you may consider it a "given" that your Boxer *knows* she is a dog and therefore will automatically get along with other dogs, this isn't always the case. Puppies that are separated from their mothers and littermates at an early age,

When pairing your Boxer with other dogs as potential playmates, keep an eye out for dogs with similar play styles. Boxers like to do a lot of high-speed shouldering, body slamming, and even some neck biting. Breeds with similar play styles include many of the sporting breeds (Labs, Goldens, German Shorthaired Pointers, and Brittanies). Other breeds that aren't as physical can and do take affront to the Boxer's highly physical play. Also, keep in mind that the Boxer's cropped ears and docked tail may be difficult for some breeds to interpret until the Boxer exhibits obvious play behaviors such as deep play bows, sideways greetings, and other friendly behaviors.

and also adults, have been shown in studies to be a bit confused about who they are and act inappropriately. Fortunately, renewed contact with other canines at an early age seems to help correct some of this behavior, but if the pup goes too long without dog-dog interactions, she may forever be fearful, mistrustful, or aggressive toward other dogs.

Likewise, adult dogs that haven't played with other dogs in a while can get a bit rusty with both expressing their intentions and interpreting those of other dogs. Except in rare cases of a truly dog-aggressive dog, most adults can find suitable playmates if their social skills are relatively intact.

Socialization from Puppyhood through Adulthood

Whether you have a puppy, an adolescent, or adult Boxer, how you choose to socialize your Boxer with other dogs will hinge around your ability to control the quality and safety of dog-dog interactions, the availability of safe playmates and groups—and particularly with (but not limited to) puppies—the risk of exposure to communicable diseases.

With that said, as pet owners have become increasingly aware of the benefits of owning a well-socialized dog, more opportunities exist for safe socialization. With dog socialization at any age, it is also important to understand and recognize the basics of your dog's body language. The principles are relatively the same for socializing a Boxer with other dogs as it is for socializing her with people: you want

Puppy classes with socialization should be segregated according to the puppy's size and age. Additionally, vaccination records should be required of all puppies. Depending on your area of the country and the risk of disease, your veterinarian may recommend that you refrain from a group puppy class until your Boxer puppy has received more than one set of vaccinations in her puppy series, so that she has less risk of contracting a deadly virus.

TRACY'S TIPS

In my opinion, the most important class in a puppy's lifelong behavioral foundation is puppy kindergarten. Don't wait six months to start training your Boxer; do it now. It's easier and more fun, and you're building a good dog network of playmates and friends for your Boxer puppy.

to keep the meetings positive and avoid any negative interactions if at all possible.

The biggest issue with dog interactions that escalate into tiffs, scuffles, or even a fight usually involve a distracted owner—one whose attention is not directed at the Boxer and her changing dog language (or increasing stress). Dog play may go from gentle to one dog becoming more aroused, and play can quickly go over the top. It's much like unsupervised children on the playground: one child gets a little rough or says something a little mean, and depending on the comfort level and temperament of the offended child, a scuffle or "words" could ensue.

The key to keeping play positive is to watch your Boxer carefully, pull her out of play if she appears to be stressed (or appears to be stressing another puppy or dog), allow her time to cool down, and then let her resume *good* play.

Some options available to Boxer owners seeking dog-dog socialization include: puppy kindergarten (puppies only); playgroups and meet-ups; and dog parks.

59

Puppy Kindergarten

In puppy kindergarten or preschool, a puppy social hour is part of the class. Typically, classes are offered for puppies as young as ten weeks and up to six months old. With leashes off and owners in the play area, the puppies of similar size and age are allowed to mix, mingle, and frolic. The class trainer is usually in the middle of the puppies, allowing the pups to play nicely and calling time-outs to keep gentle play from going over the top and becoming a squabble.

Gentle Adults

A friendly, adult dog that is fully vaccinated can be a great playmate and teacher for your puppy. Just be sure, however, that the dog is indeed friendly and very tolerant of puppy antics. A bad experience with a dog, such as an attack that sends your puppy screaming for help under your legs, can cause your puppy to be fearful of other dogs, even as an adult. Keep things positive, keep things in control, and keep things safe for your puppy. If you follow these rules, your Boxer should be able to continue the rules of canines and grow into a sociable dog.

Playgroups and Meet-ups

These groups are usually made up of Boxers and generally require proof of vaccinations for participation. (If a group doesn't require this, make sure your pup is fully vaccinated before participating.) Boxer playgroups and meet-ups can be found by checking Yahoo, Craigslist, Meet-up.com, and various social networking sites. Playgroups and meet-ups typically meet once a month in someone's large, fenced backyard or at a nearby dog park. In order to be in the group, Boxers must not be dog-aggressive, and owners usually are good about closely supervising their dogs' play.

With a puppy, be very careful to limit her play to very gentle adult Boxers and other puppies. Sometimes allowing a younger puppy to play with the big guys (who can get pretty physical) can be overwhelming, even if the adult dogs are not bullying the pup.

With an adult Boxer, watch interactions carefully and watch for overheating during summer months.

Dog Parks

Until your puppy has reached her adult size, dog parks are not advisable. Adult dogs with inattentive owners may gang up on a puppy or simply play too roughly. Wait until your Boxer has some size to her and make sure she's fully vaccinated. In addition, the following are a few tips to keep dog park encounters safe and positive for your Boxer.

1. **Visit the park during non-peak hours.** Fewer people (and dogs) are using the park. There's less risk of a squabble, and it allows you to supervise your dog's interactions more closely.
2. **Use the bull-pen area.** Take your Boxer off the leash in this fenced entry area and allow all the dogs in the

larger play area to meet and greet your boxer through the fence. There should be *no* signs of aggression through the fence.

3. **Time your dog's entry.** Once the dogs have become disinterested in your dog and have gone back to playing, *then* let your Boxer in the park. Walk into the park with your Boxer.

4. **Keep moving.** Most arguments occur between dogs when owners socialize on the edge of the play area and stop watching the interactions between the dogs. Some dogs will play just fine but usually there's one that will push the envelope. Play goes over the top, a dog gets offended, and trouble ensues. To avoid this, move through the park constantly and keep your Boxer moving. (Hey! It's great exercise for you, too!)

5. **Take time-outs.** Good playmates will break from the play and lie down, calming the play of the group. If your dog doesn't relax on her own, call her out and help her calm down before rejoining the group.

6. **Trust your gut.** If you feel play is going over the top or if you feel your Boxer shows signs of being stressed (she is being chased and not returning the chase, she has a piloerection while running away, her body language is that of a stressed dog), remove her from play. Don't believe other owners who say, "Oh, just let them play!" or, "They're fine!" Invariably, these are the same people whose dogs *do* bite or are the playground bullies. Trust your instincts and avoid trouble and potential injury.

On-Leash Meetings with Other Dogs

In a perfect dog world, your Boxer would be able to meet other dogs off leash through a barrier, such as a wire fence or a dog gate. This type of meeting gives a less outgoing dog or puppy the ability to make the approach to the other dog as she feels comfortable. The barrier allows the dogs to meet each other with friendly behaviors (and get all that sniffing accomplished), with both dogs having the ability to create more space by backing away from the fence if she feels threatened by the other dog or is stressed for any other reason. Once the dogs have met each other, then they can play together—supervised—in an enclosure. Off leash, dogs are able to produce more natural, friendly behaviors without the restriction of a leash: deep play bows, approaching indirectly (an arcing approach), nose-to-

rear circling, lifting paws, twisting, rolling sideways, face licking, back rolling, etc. All these moves are more easily done when not on a leash.

That's not to say that puppies and dogs that are on a leash can't have good meetings with other dogs, but they are more challenging for the owner because the Boxer's movements are restrained. To help your Boxer make friendly meetings with other dogs while on leash, the following are suggestions to make on-leash meetings positive experiences.

1. **Watch your dog's body language.** What kind of behaviors is she showing? Is she showing any signs of being stressed? If so, call your Boxer back to you and give her a little more space.

2. **Look for rude greeting behaviors.** Direct head-on approaches, staring, jumping up toward dog, barking in the other dog's face, putting a muzzle over the dogs shoulders and holding this position, preventing the dog from sniffing rear ends, and, of course, any aggressive body language—usually characterized by stiff, erect body posture and a stiff, high tail carriage (don't be fooled by a wagging tail!)—are all rude greeting behaviors between dogs. If the dog your Boxer is meeting displays these behaviors, call your Boxer to you to avoid a confrontation.

3. **Resist pulling back on your dog.** As noted in number 2, a rude behavior is rearing back on the dog's hind legs, which is often caused accidently when you pull back hard on the Boxer's leash. Try to call your dog out of a meeting or slow her down with better leash train-

ing. A dog that rushes up to another dog can also be very intimidating and upsetting to the recipient dog.

4. **Allow the leash to be slack.** A tightened leash sends an automatic signal to your Boxer that you are concerned. This can translate into your Boxer being concerned with meeting the other dog (i.e., why is my owner so worried about this other dog?). Again, work on good leash training skills to control an exuberant Boxer and prevent a "rude" greeting by an otherwise friendly dog.

5. **Walk side-by-side.** Before allowing two dogs to meet, particularly if one is a bit timid or one is a bit exuberant, walk with the other owner and his or her dog side-by-side for 10 or 20 minutes. Observe how the dogs react or don't react to each other. Total disinterest is fine; allow the dogs to meet each other when they are both calm and used to each other.

Handling Leash Aggression

If you work with your Boxer as a puppy and she is a confident and well-socialized dog as an adult, you will most likely never have issues with leash aggression. If your Boxer is a bit timid and/or isn't well socialized with other dogs, you may be at higher risk for leash aggression. Dog-aggressive Boxers can also be leash aggressive, but typically a dog-aggressive Boxer will be aggressive toward other dogs both on and off the leash, whereas the leash-aggressive Boxer will only display aggression when on leash (when she can't escape) and may

Prong collars are very effective if used appropriately and without malice. If a head halter or a no-pull harness will work, try these tools first. If these tools don't work, then a prong collar might be recommended on a temporary basis. Prong collars are fitted so they are snug and the actual wearing of the collar does not hurt the Boxer. Discomfort only occurs when the Boxer pulls against you (i.e., when the Boxer lunges at an oncoming dog). When the Boxer pulls, the prongs tighten, and the dog immediately backs off to avoid discomfort. This is negative reinforcement in that the dog changes his behavior to avoid the discomfort of the prong collar. If you are considering using a prong collar, remember that it is not a permanent "fix": you will need to solve the problem of the leash aggression itself. What the prong collar can offer is immediate control and the ability to work on the source of the behavior problem. The ultimate goal is to return to a quick release or buckle collar.

only display aggression to certain breeds, sizes, or more dominant dogs.

So, what exactly is leash aggression?

Leash aggression describes the behavior of a dog when she is on leash and is either meeting another dog or coming within close range of another dog. Rather than display relaxed, friendly behaviors or non-interest in the other dog, the Boxer becomes stressed and agitated. She may bark, growl, lunge, and otherwise act like a complete fool.

Do not be embarrassed! This is a situation that at best you can solve, and at the very least, you can make manageable. But, you need to invest some time and effort into working with your Boxer. Whatever you do, don't stop walking your Boxer; start walking her *smarter*. Here's how:

1. **Give her space.** Determine how far away from other dogs you need to be for your Boxer to pass another dog without causing a commotion. You want her to be relaxed. For some dogs, this may be several yards away. For other dogs, this may be across the street. Know what your Boxer's comfort zone is (where she shows relaxed dog language and friendly behaviors), and start with this distance.

2. **Keep it loose.** If your Boxer is leash-aggressive, you're likely to be self-conscious about your dog's behavior. Boxers can look and sound awful when they want to and this is precisely their goal when they exhibit leash aggression. If you've got a stranglehold of your Boxer *before she starts pulling and lunging on the leash*, your nervousness about what is about to happen as you approach another dog will make your Boxer more anxious and more reactive. Try to leave a little slack in the leash, but keep the leash short. (Do not use a retractable leash with a leash-aggressive dog! A four-foot leash is optimal.)

What If My Boxer is Truly Dog-aggressive?

A truly dog-aggressive Boxer is not very common, but it can occur. Though generally not a danger to people (unless other forms of aggression are present), a dog-aggressive Boxer is a hazard to other dogs and a liability to the Boxer owner. Unlike the leash-aggressive dog that acts "big" because she is, in reality, afraid of the other dog and will settle down as soon as the offending dog is far enough away (the comfort zone), the dog-aggressive Boxer often will not settle down and will continue to try to go after the other dog. Most importantly, if the dog-aggressive Boxer breaks free of her owner, she will go after the other dog—as opposed to the leash aggressive, timid dog, which will not attack the other dog.

Because of the safety issues of a dog-aggressive Boxer, you must make sure that your Boxer is in complete control at all times; you can work toward this with extensive obedience training. (Select a skilled trainer or training school—one that is willing to work with you and your Boxer through her dog-aggression issues.) You will want your Boxer to be so well trained that she can perform all basic exercises (see Chapter 8) with consistency and utmost reliability. Teach your Boxer a rock solid down (see page 103) and use it! It's very difficult for a dog to bark when she is in a down. If your Boxer is an intact male dog, neuter him; this can help (but it is not a guarantee). Continue to work on exercises to diminish your Boxer's leash aggression tendencies through the training methods mentioned here, and remember: You bought this dog to be your companion. Maybe she's not the best around other dogs and maybe she won't be able to be the life of a dog park but, if she is an amazing family dog and a loving companion, it's worth the effort to make her controllable and predictable around other dogs.

3. **Have control.** When a full-grown Boxer launches herself against a leash and a flat buckle collar, you may feel as if you can barely hang on to her. This can add to your stress. In addition to working on obedience so that she listens to you better and you have greater control, use a head collar (head halter) or a no-pull harness to provide instant control, or consider a prong collar for strong, heavy pullers with serious aggression issues.

4. **Distract her.** To keep her from focusing on the other dog, distract her with a series of obedience exercises, such as a series of fast *sits* and *downs*, or a fast *heel*, a *recall*, or any other combination of exercises. (See Chapter 8.) Do not reward her with treats or let her play with a toy unless she is focused on you and *not* the other dog.

5. **Reward her for relaxed behaviors.** If you are walking past another dog and your Boxer is showing calm, friendly behaviors (and remember, you may be across the street or 10 feet [3 m] away), *do* reward her with verbal praise and, if you'd like, treats. If she has shown any negative behaviors, make sure she has shown relaxed behaviors for at *least three* seconds or more. If you reward her too soon, she will associate the reward with the inappropriate, aggressive behaviors and not the calm, relaxed body language—and you'll end up creating a far worse problem.

6. **Ignore bad behaviors.** Resist the urge to yell or shout at your Boxer when she *does* show aggressive behaviors. Your shouting will further excite her and drive her to worse behaviors. Don't go there. *Remove her from the situation*. Quickly. Calmly. Firmly.

7. **Walk *away*.** Even if this isn't the direction you are going, make your Boxer turn away from the other dog that has upset her. Turning away from the dog (even if this is sideways or 90 degrees) does not allow the Boxer to feel she has successfully "driven" the other dog away. Just as barking at the delivery man at the front door and watching him go back to his truck makes a Boxer think she has "won," barking at another dog and making the other dog turn away may have the same effect.

8. **Avoid any and all situations.** Every time your Boxer behaves badly on leash, it will require more work—perhaps weeks of more work on your part—to squelch or at least lessen her leash aggression, so know your Boxer. Know her body language so you can tell when she is transitioning from relaxed, calm behaviors to stressful, fearful, or aggressive behaviors. Know what your Boxer's comfort zone is and how much distance you need to give her for her to be void of aggressive behaviors. You can only prevent leash aggression if you can prevent your Boxer from becoming anxious or stressed while on leash.

9. **Work to get closer.** As your Boxer consistently walks by other dogs quietly and relaxed, work to gradually lessen the space between your Boxer and the other dog. If your Boxer needs to be across the street to be comfortable, work to walk a yard closer. If your Boxer needs to be 10 feet (3 m) away

to be relaxed, try to narrow this to 9 feet (2.7 m), and then 8 feet (2.4 m), with the goal of eventually being able to walk by within a yard of another dog and owner.

The Boxer as a Second Dog

Many dog owners mistakenly believe that all dogs get along and that by adding a second dog, the two dogs will be best buddies. Sometimes this happens, and sometimes it doesn't. And sometimes, if a squabble ensues between dogs, a lifelong grudge can develop that requires permanent separation.

So, whether you're bringing a puppy or an adult Boxer into a home with a resident dog, you'll want to set up the situation for success. At a minimum, you'll want the two dogs to tolerate each other (dogs that

When driving with a new Boxer, crate both the resident and the new Boxer. Do not allow the dogs to be loose together in a moving car. You will have no way to control their interactions—which can develop into a dangerous driving situation, not to mention a negative interaction between the dogs!

ignore each other are fine). If you're really lucky, the new Boxer and our resident dog will bond and will become best buds.

So, how do you introduce your new Boxer to the resident dog? Carefully and slowly.

Puppies

When the new Boxer is a puppy, don't assume the resident dog will love the little one. Not all adult dogs like puppies. Older dogs may not like the fast movement or the crying, or they may be worried about getting bumped or knocked down. Other adult dogs may like the puppy but may overwhelm the little Boxer. Here are a few tips to making the transition to adding a new Boxer a little easier:

1. **Set up a barrier.** Keep the puppy and resident dog physically separated. Use an exercise pen or a dog gate between rooms to keep the two dogs apart, but allow them to check each other out.
2. **Supervise.** Even with the gate or an x-pen in place, watch the two dogs carefully. If either puppy or adult shows signs of stress, separate them even

further. Crate the puppy or the adult dog for a little while. And remember, these barriers are not totally safe and can be jumped over or knocked down by the adult dog.

3. **Play with the resident dog.** Make him feel special with extra attention. It's very easy to neglect the older dog with a new puppy in the house.

Three's a Pack?

If you increase your dog family from two to three dogs, you will increase the complexity of keeping the peace among your resident dogs. Though many dog experts have varying theories regarding pack dynamics in domestic dogs, little research has been performed on this subject. Basically, you've taken a stable, two-dog family and added a third dimension. You've got many of the same cautions as a director of a doggie daycare might have. Make the introductions of the newest family member in the same way as a new second dog, and watch the behaviors and body language of all dogs closely. Because dogs in a "pack" (defined as more than two dogs) do tend to attack a dog that shows weakness (even within a family of dogs), the risk of possible injury from a squabble becomes a bit higher with three dogs, rather than two. (Though two dogs can get into terrible fights on their own…)

---

4. **Divide meals.** If the puppy is being fed three times a day, portion your adult dog's food for three portions, too. Don't let him feel as if the puppy is getting more rewards than he is. Food is a precious resource among dogs. Also, consider giving your resident dog some new toys, too. Some people say dogs can't count, but they seem to be cognizant of the fact that a puppy has a pile of toys and they don't…

5. **Watch for relaxed behaviors.** Only allow physical interaction between the puppy and the adult dog when the resident dog is comfortable with the puppy and is being friendly and calm at the barrier. *This could take a few hours, a day, or in some cases, weeks.* Don't rush this part!

6. **Unsupervised dogs must be separated.** Even when everything seems rosy between the puppy and the adult dog, do not allow the puppy and adult dog to be together unsupervised. Some Boxer owners always crate their dogs when they leave the house and never leave them together unsupervised.

7. **Trust your instincts.** Observe body language closely, and remember: a lack of friendly, relaxed behavior is a transition to stress, fear, or aggression. Also, mixed signals—friendly and fearful behaviors, for example—are a sign of stress, too. Don't ignore these behaviors. Separate the dogs and allow them to become comfortable again.

Adult Dogs

If you are adopting a Boxer as a second pet, the Boxer rescue most likely has

> *Note: This separation phase may last a few days or may need to go as long as a few weeks. Many adopted dogs fail in a multi-pet home when the dogs are not given enough time to adjust to each other.*

already worked with you in introducing the new Boxer to your resident dog to help make sure they will get along. If you are rescuing a Boxer form a shelter, you may not have had this luxury. If this is the case, you can still make a smooth transition by using many of the same principles you would use if introducing a puppy into a resident dog household—but with a few more cautions.

1. **Introduce the dogs on neutral territory.** Have a family member take the resident dog on a walk at a local park, for example. Bring the new dog to the park and walk side-by-side for 30 minutes or more. The goal is to have both dogs showing comfortable relaxed body language.

2. **Walk the dogs regularly.** Each dog should have a walker from the family. Try to walk the dogs at least two to three times a day. Watch for any transitioning from relaxed behavior to fear or stress. If one of the dogs becomes stressed, create a little more room between the dogs.

3. **Separate and supervise.** Double-stack dog gates to create a virtually unjumpable barrier between the adult dogs—but do supervise their interactions at the gate. Allow the dogs to

see each other and sniff but not touch. Watch carefully for signs of stress so that you can create more space before there are any signs of aggression. When you can't watch the dogs, crate them.

4. **Supervise all physical interaction closely.** Only allow contact between the dogs if the daily walks and supervised separation show no sign of stress and the dogs either ignore each other or are friendly. For the first physical interaction, allow the dogs to interact for a short period, 5 to 10 minutes, preferably after a long walk. If all goes well, you can allow the dogs several interactions in a day, increasing the time together slowly, and only if all goes well. If there's stress, go back to supervised separation and frequent walks for a day or more before trying again.

5. **Spoil the resident dog.** He's having to share your time and affection now with another dog. Make sure he's busy, tired (lots of exercise!), and has lots of time with you. A new toy for crate time wouldn't hurt either. All of these things will help for the resident dog to associate good things with the presence of the new dog—not a loss of good things.

6. **Crate, crate, crate.** Even when the dogs seem to be friendly and get along, remember—your presence is in part the reason for this calm. When you leave the home, you are no longer in charge. The dogs could squabble (with disastrous results) or, in a better scenario, the two could become destructive (i.e., what one doesn't think of, the other will). So, crate your dogs whenever you can't be home and/or can't supervise the dogs' interactions.

7. Be patient. Introducing a new dog into a home smoothly may take one week, or it may take six weeks. Your efforts, however, will be rewarded with a balanced dog family . . . eventually.

Note: If your Boxer puppy is the second dog in your family, be sure to never leave the puppy alone with the adult dog. Many adult dogs are fairly tolerant of puppies, but some dogs are not. Initially, you'll want to supervise their time together and make sure the adult dog accepts the puppy as a member of the family.

Socializing Your Adult Dog with Other Dogs

Though your Boxer's attitude may be somewhat set as to how she views other canines, if you've adopted a sociable Boxer, she will benefit mentally and physically from playing with other dogs. As with a puppy, it is important to screen your Boxer's playmates and make sure they are healthy and not bullies. Always supervise her play just to make sure no one accidently gets hurt. If you frequent a dog park where the dogs are allowed

to play off leash in a fenced-in area, don't assume that all dogs are friendly. Get to know the folks who frequent the park and meet their dogs before you bring your Boxer out to play.

If you're the one with the bully (see Dog-dog Aggression, page 92), it would be advisable to work on control exercises, such as putting the dog in a *sit* (see *Sit*, page 99) when on walks to prevent lunging, or even a *down* (see *Down*, page 103) for more control. Keep in mind that animal behaviorists feel that dog-dog aggression is perhaps one of the most treatable forms of aggression and that if you are willing to work with your dog, you can make inroads into better behavior.

> Before allowing physical interaction (play!), be sure to clear out all toys and any potential items that might be seen as toys. It is very easy for dogs to squabble over prized possessions.

6 *Habituation*

We often feel that the sights and sounds of our home, neighborhood, and lifestyles are something that our canine companions will readily adapt to and take in stride. We see this happen every day with puppies. Naturally inquisitive, Boxer puppies often will "check out" a new sound or thing. They'll listen, look, and, if nothing happens (and you don't appear to be worried or frightened), they will most likely ignore the "event" the next time it occurs.

For example, the first time your Boxer puppy hears the sound of the dishwasher, he will most likely run over to see what's happening. After thoroughly checking out the situation and determining there is no danger, the next time you turn on the dishwasher he will most likely ignore the event, or at least not be alarmed by it.

This process of learning everyday life events is called *habituation*. And most often, as mentioned in the above example, everything goes smoothly. There are some everyday events, however, that you'll want to practice to make sure they become an easy part of your Boxer's life.

When Something Is Scary

On occasion, things don't go well and your Boxer may show a fearful response to something. It is particularly important during these inappropriate responses to know how to respond so that he will not be frightened in the future.

The biggest mistake you can make when your Boxer is frightened by something, such as a siren, a flapping awning, or a thunderstorm, is to do what we humans are genetically programmed to do: comfort him. Resist the urge to hold him, pet him, or otherwise try to reassure him by saying, "*It's all right.*" Though we see ourselves as comforting the dog, the Boxer sees this attention as a reward for his behavior. In other words, instead of taking action to decrease the frightened behavior, we have actually rewarded the dog for his behavior and have begun the cycle of positive reinforcement—but for the *wrong* behavior. Oops.

So, what should you do? First, if something unsettles your Boxer initially, don't make a big deal about it. A fearful, timid, or even startled response can be quite normal when the "something" or event is big and noisy, or something he has never heard or seen before. If you remain calm and settled, he will look to you and take in your response. The next time he is exposed to the scary noise or thing (i.e., a garbage truck), you will most likely find him a bit bolder. However, if you tense up in anticipation of his freaking out over a sight or sound, he will read your anticipation and it

fire station, try to set him up for success and reward him when he behaves calmly. In other words, if you hear sirens, don't rush your dog out to the curb and force him to be close to the very thing that he fears. Instead, when you hear sirens outside, and your Boxer happens to be behaving normally (no fear) reward him with a treat. As he becomes more used to the sound in the home, you can gradually take him outside but far away from the sound, and reward as noted above. Basically, the more opportunities you have to reward him for good behavior, the more likely he is to overcome his phobias.

Desensitizing

Another method of allaying fears and phobias involves desensitizing the dog. For example, if your Boxer is deathly afraid of thunderstorms, some animal behaviorists have had success with playing thunderstorm tapes at low levels in the home regularly when there aren't any storms. In this way, the dog becomes accustomed to the sound of the storms and realizes that nothing bad happens to him. Positive reinforcement comes into play because when the dog doesn't pace, whine, bark, drool profusely, or pant, something very good will happen—a treat. Desensitizing works in the same basic way as positive rewards except that desensitizing provides many more exposures to the feared event—in this case, a thunderstorm—and subsequently, many more opportunities to catch the dog behaving appropriately and to reward him.

Of course, not all Boxers respond to desensitization training, particularly with

is almost *guaranteed* that he will respond exactly as you don't want him to.

So, how do you habituate a dog that has already shown that he has some apprehensions about something? There are four ways to work with this situation, and depending on your Boxer and the particular circumstances, one method may work better than another.

The Power of Positive Rewards

It is important to reward your Boxer when he does behave appropriately. For example, if he is apprehensive about the fire trucks that roar out of your neighborhood

thunderstorms. (Some theorize that what triggers panic in dogs is the change in the atmosphere.) Several products are available for dogs with storm anxiety; they have been reported to have varying levels of success but might be worth a try:

1. **Rescue Remedy**—this is a natural, flower essence remedy. It is available in a pet formula that is alcohol free. Typically, four drops are applied to the anxious dog's gums.
2. **D.A.P.**—Dog Appeasing Pheromone mimics the pheromones produced by a lactating female dog. This product can be sprayed on the dogs bedding or used as a plug-in diffuser. In clinical trials with D.A.P., destructive behavior and vocalization (excessive barking and whining) were reported to have improved or been resolved by 72 percent, and 85 percent, respectively.
3. **Wraps**—the Thunder Shirt and Anxiety Wrap are two products that can be worn by dogs to help calm them during thunderstorms. The theory behind these wraps is that constant pressure has a calming effect on the nervous system and can relieve anxiety (much like swaddling a crying baby).

Removing the Stimulus

Sure, you can spend weeks and months working to have your Boxer overcome certain fears, but in some cases, it's much simpler to remove the cause of the fear. For example, with a dog who is deathly afraid of helium balloons, the easiest way to solve the problem is to take the offending balloons out of your Boxer's

> **TRACY'S TIPS**
> You can buy desensitization CDs for specific sounds, such as fireworks, that you can play at low levels and gradually build to normal volume. Reward only when your Boxer is showing good behaviors, and remember that your demeanor means a lot. if you don't react to the sounds, your Boxer will learn not to react, too.

sight and into another room. Have a Boxer that's afraid of vacuums? Maybe it's simpler to crate him while you clean.

Adapting the Stimulus

Sometimes you can't remove something that is causing your Boxer to behave inappropriately, but you can change the "thing" so that it no longer causes a problem. For example, some adopted Boxers have never seen a large, plate glass window or a screen and will literally try to barge right through them. Unfortunately, this can be quite dangerous.

In the adapting method, the situation is resolved by placing a piece of duct tape (or painter's tape that can be removed later) diagonally across the screen or window. The placement of the tape allows the dog to "see" the screen or glass and will discourage the dog from trying to jump through the window or door. With time, you should be able to remove the tape and your Boxer will still respect your screens and sliding doors.

Home Schooling

Everyday Life Habits to Work On

When you bring your Boxer puppy home, he will most likely be quite congenial with everything you want to do with him. The trick is to *keep* him this way! The following are some of the daily living skills your Boxer will need to learn to accept, but that many owners forget to work on. If you wait until you *need* to do these things, you will most likely find yourself in a losing battle with a full-grown Boxer, so start early and keep at it!

Toenail Clipping

■ When your puppy is very little, you can use a cat claw clipper or a small dog clipper to trim his toenails. Take only a tiny piece off when you clip, being careful not to "quick" him, or cut the nail too short, which will make the nail bleed.

■ Practice even if he doesn't need it. Make it a habit to handle your puppy's paws every day and even pretend to clip his nails by touching the clipper to his nails.

■ Reward good Boxers with a treat for every toenail. You can gradually fade the treats to every paw, and then after clipping all four paws' nails as he becomes used to the procedure.

■ Distract him. Have another person rub his ears or belly to help distract him and help to make the toenail clipping experience a pleasant one.

■ Older dogs: If you have an adult Boxer that doesn't like his toenails clipped, begin slowly. Clip one toenail, reward him, and let him be. Try for a toenail a day. Arthritic Boxers may be uncomfortable standing on three legs for nail clipping. Have someone help support your older dog while you trim, or encourage your Boxer to lie down during nail clippings.

■ Practice and use the *stand-stay* or *down-stay*. (See *Stay* page 101.) Wriggly adult dogs will do well during toenail clipping if they are solid on these commands.

Teeth Care

■ With your puppy in your lap, use a finger brush with a little dab of dog toothpaste—*never* use human toothpaste—and rub your puppy's teeth.

■ When he accepts this, you can move to a toothbrush. Remember, he will have a natural tendency while he is teething to try to chew the brush. Have patience!

■ Adult dogs can be taught to have their teeth brushed, too. With apprehensive dogs, take baby steps. Use a finger brush to begin with and work on his teeth for only a few seconds, rewarding good behavior with a treat.

■ Teaching the *sit-stay* (see *Sit*, page 99) can help immensely with dental care!

Grooming

- Most Boxers enjoy being brushed, particularly if you begin when they are puppies.
- Try to make brushing a daily part of your puppy's care regime—not because he necessarily needs it, but because it will get him used to it. Use a rubber zoomgroom and grooming becomes a massage session, which is a reward in itself!

Baths

- As with brushing and toenail clipping, your Boxer may not need baths on such a regular basis, but if you don't get him used to water and enjoying his baths, you could find yourself struggling with 60 pounds (27 kg) of muscle that *doesn't* want to get wet. So if possible, rinse your Boxer in warm water every two weeks.
- Make bathtime enjoyable. Use warm water and bathe him outside only if the temperature is warm. When bathing inside in the tub, make sure you have a towel on the bottom of it so that he won't slip. Do you have a self-service dog wash in your area? If so, go! Employees will help you get your Boxer in the washtub, and you won't have to clean out your own bathtub. Dog wash employees are typically pretty dog-savvy and can offer great opportunities for added socialization for your Boxer.
- Older dogs can learn, too. If you have an adult dog that hasn't had a bath,

or is very resistant to the idea, start slowly. Put just a little water in the tub and try to entice him in with a toy, or step in the tub yourself and see if he'll join you. If this fails, put his back legs in first and then coax the rest of his body into the tub. Don't make him stay in too long the first time and reward him for good behavior with a treat. Gradually increase the time he spends in the tub until you can actually give him a bath.

- Work on his *stand-stay* (see *Stand*, page 111). If he is solid in his commands, he will be more likely to tolerate a bath. You can then work on actually helping him to enjoy them . . .

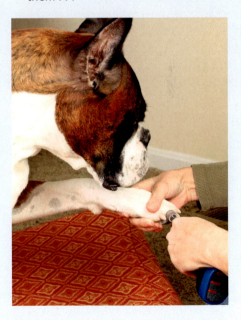

The Adult Boxer

Many times a rescued or adopted adult Boxer may need more work in the habituation department than a young puppy. Often, they have led a rather dismal life, relegated to the backyard with minimal indoor time. If he comes from such a background, you should expect to have to show him the "ropes" at home, in the yard, and around the neighborhood.

You may find that the newly rescued Boxer will tag along behind you wherever you go in the home, which is actually a great way to habituate your dog to your lifestyle and home. Your fearless reactions to the sights and sounds of your house will be picked up by your Boxer. You can expect to see a few startled expressions as he encounters new experiences. Common "new" experiences can include learning to negotiate slick floors, not being startled by the sound of kitchen appliances (i.e., dishwashers, ice makers, blenders), and figuring out how to climb stairs one step at a time instead of trying to jump them all at once.

You'll find that adult Boxers are ready learners, and with patience, practice, and praise, your adult Boxer will begin settling into your home within a matter of days. Those adopted dogs that have had the benefit of a loving family and many good experiences will often walk into your home, survey the situation briefly, and then begin acting as if they've lived with you all their lives.

The key to habituating the adult Boxer is to anticipate that there will be many new experiences for him. Work steadfastly at establishing his trust in you, and introducing him gradually and gently to the sights and sounds of your home, yard, and neighborhood.

TRACY'S TIPS

Using a nail grinder can be safer for nail clipping, as it doesn't leave rough edges that can catch and rip. Since it acts as a file, and since the nail grinder takes only small bits of nail off at a time, you're far less likely to quick your dog. Acclimating the Boxer to the sound and smell of the grinder is worth the effort. Start with just the sound first and reward good behaviors. Once the Boxer is comfortable with the sound, acclimate him to the feel and smell of the actual nail filing.

Habituating to the Crate

Crates aren't just for house-training! If your Boxer is acclimated to a crate, the crate can be added to your arsenal of training tools—not only for house-training, but also for calming time-outs, a safe spot for when you're not home, travel (both in the car and in the "hold," if traveling by air), and separation anxiety (see page 79). So, whether you own a puppy or an adult Boxer—one of your first priorities should be to acclimate him to a crate. You want the crate to be a source of comfort

> *A crate should never be used as punishment. It should always be a safe haven for your Boxer.*

for the Boxer, a place where he can relax and feel safe.

Some Boxers will take immediately to the crate, particularly a puppy that has had a little crate time at the breeder's home prior to coming to live with you, or a rescue dog that has spent time at a foster parent's house, where acclimating to a crate is a first priority. If your Boxer hasn't had any crate experience or is a bit leery of the whole concept, the following steps will help get your Boxer comfortable with his crate.

1. **Put the crate in a central location in the home.** Boxers love their families and need to be in the center of all activities. If a Boxer can see you at all times, he's more likely to be willing to rest in his crate.
2. **Make it comfy.** The bedding should be clean, dry, and soft. If you don't know if your Boxer is a shredder, or if house-training is still a work in progress, you may want to opt for lining the crate with pee pads or newspapers. Also, make sure that the crate is in a warm place in the winter and a cool place in the summer.
3. **Keep the door open.** Allow the Boxer to investigate the crate on his own. If he needs encouragement, toss a cookie in the back of the crate. If the door won't stay open, or if the Boxer

is a bit nervous about the door itself, remove the door or fasten it open.
4. **Associate good things with the crate.** Feed your Boxer in his crate. Give him his favorite, safe chew bones and treats while in his crate. These "busy chews" serve a dual purpose: they are a reward for going in the crate *and* they keep the Boxer calmly occupied while he is in the crate.
5. **Go topless.** If your Boxer is fearful of a two-piece, plastic crate (and won't even go in to eat or retrieve a snack), remove the top half of the crate and make an open bed for the Boxer. As your Boxer becomes more comfortable with the bottom shell of his crate, add the top half (securely!) and then, finally, the door. Or, consider purchasing a wire crate, which will have a more open feeling for the Boxer.

Home Schooling

Teaching Your Boxer the Ropes

If you spend some time introducing your Boxer to your home, yard, neighborhood, and lifestyle activities in a positive way, he will likely settle into your family with no great problems. The best way to do this is to include him as a member of the family from day one.

- Take your Boxer everywhere you can in the car. Try to associate car trips with something more than a visit to the veterinarian's office! Maybe a frolic in the local dog park or a lick from an ice cream cone?
- Carsickness is often a nervous response to travel, so the more trips you make, typically the less nervous your Boxer will become over time. Always use a crate and make sure he is never left in a hot car.
- Carry treats with you so you can reward him for good responses no matter where you are. As your puppy or dog becomes more used to the sights and sounds in your neighborhood, you won't need to treat as much, but lots of praise and hands-on attention are always great rewards.
- If you have any particular lifestyle situations that you want to include your Boxer in, such as boating or visiting the beach, make sure you begin including him at a young age and keep things very positive!
- Don't rush him. Recognize when he is experiencing genuine fear, and work with him in a patient, positive manner.
- In severe cases of phobias, consider consulting a certified animal behaviorist or a veterinary animal behaviorist for advice.

6. **Exercise your Boxer.** A tired Boxer is more likely to relax and maybe even sleep in a crate or seek out a little quiet time.

7. **Consider calming aids.** One particular product that has shown success in calming stressed dogs is D.A.P.—Dog Appeasing Pheromone. This synthetic substance mimics the pheromones of a lactating female dog. It is a calming scent that dogs never seem to forget. D.A.P. is sold over the counter and can be sprayed on the dog's bedding or used as a diffuser in the room where the crate is placed.

8. **Don't give up!** Keep working with your Boxer. Go slowly—particularly if your Boxer is afraid of the crate. (A panicked, crated dog *can* injure himself!) Minimize stress and keep building positive experiences with the crate.

Separation Anxiety

Boxers do not like to be left behind. As a working dog that loves his people, his happiest moments are those spent with you. Leaving him behind is stressful *for him*. This may make the Boxer perhaps a little more susceptible to separation anxiety (or SA) than other more independent breeds.

If your Boxer becomes excessively stressed, anxious, or panicked when you leave the home and can't be crated because he is a hazard to himself (i.e., he breaks teeth, damages paws, pulls nails out, urinates and spins, and/or defecates when trying to get out), then he could very well be suffering from separation anxiety or SA.

Diagnosing SA

Often, adult Boxers are assumed to have SA but really don't. True SA is triggered by the behaviors (yours) that the dog recognizes as signals that you are about to leave him. Actions such as picking up your keys, putting on a coat, grabbing a book bag or purse, or locking a back door will start anxious responses in the Boxer, such as drooling, whining, panting, pacing, or barking.

These anxious responses only signify SA *if they don't stop shortly after you've left*. The SA dog will continue to display these behaviors until you return home and may add other destructive behaviors to the list, such as tearing down blinds, gutting upholstery, chewing through drywall, scratching doors, defecating, and urinating.

SA Resource
Perhaps one of the best guidebooks to working a dog through separation anxiety is a pamphlet by Patricia McConnell, Ph.D., entitled I'll Be Home Soon: How to Prevent and Treat Separation Anxiety (McConnell Publishing, Ltd., June 1, 2000). The book is only 38 pages; however, it details different methods for pre- vention of SA as well as a 6-week training plan for the severest cases of separation anxiety.

If you suspect your Boxer has SA, set up an audio or video recorder—or webcam— and *see* what he does once you've left. You might be surprised to see that your Boxer settles down for a snooze. Or, if he's bored (or needs more exercise), he goes looking for items to chew or shred. The body language of the dog is key (see Body Language Primer, page 49). If the Boxer is relaxed but is looking for trouble, that is not separation anxiety. If the Boxer is stressed for the duration of your absence, this most likely *is* SA.

True SA can range from mild to extreme but all levels can be treated. Dogs can learn to relax while you're gone but it takes commitment from the owner for up to a 6-week period. The more severe the SA, the more important it is for the owner to make this training commitment. The benefits of a dog that is able to relax while his owner is gone extends beyond having a calmer household but is also invaluable to both the dog and owner's mental health!

Prevention

Before we cover how to lessen a dog's SA, let's start with preventing it in the first place. From the moment you bring your puppy home, prepare him for separation. Typically, families will bring a puppy home over a long weekend, a spring or winter break, or summer vacation. Everyone is home 24/7 during this time with the young puppy. It's a Boxer's *dream*. Imagine, though, the little guy's surprise when vacation is over or school starts and suddenly the pup is (gasp!) *alone*. This could be his first experience ever with being alone.

First, acclimate him to his crate and begin this as soon as you bring him home (see page 76). He should feel safe and secure in his crate. This will help immensely when you're gone.

Second, leave him but leave him occupied. Yes, you'll want to take him everywhere with you, but it is equally important that you carve out a little time for leaving him alone. You can crate or pen him with a great chew toy and walk into another room. Leave him on his own for 5 to 10 minutes and then return. Leave him for longer periods, too, being sure to carefully follow a solid house-training schedule (see Chapter 4, House-training), so he never soils his crate.

Third, be sure to exercise him before leaving. He's tired, he's had an opportunity to relieve himself, he's got a busy chew in his crate (kinda like a pacifier), and he's now primed to associate relaxing in the crate.

Fourth and finally, don't make a big fuss over him when you leave or return. Treat it as a matter of fact, and leave with an air of confidence that your Boxer will be just fine while you're gone. He'll sense this confidence and the fact that you're not anxious (which can cause him to be anxious).

Mild to Moderate Separation Anxiety

If you didn't have the opportunity to *prevent* your Boxer from developing SA, and you've recorded his behaviors while you're gone (and ruled out lack of exercise, boredom, too much freedom, lack of house-training, illness such as a urinary tract infection, and other possible causes for certain behaviors), the following are some guidelines that can help mild to moderate cases of SA.

1. **Use a crate.** The SA dog needs a place where he can feel safe and secure while you're gone. If he's not acclimated to the crate, work on this skill with him. If he is fine in a crate while you're home but panicks to the point of urinating, defecating, or is at risk of injuring himself by trying to bite or claw his way out of the crate, *this is not a mild or moderate case of SA*. Do not crate this dog. (See Extreme SA, page 82).

the back door. Turn on lights, turn off lights. Open and shut doors. When your dog shows relaxed behaviors during these moments, reward him with praise and a treat. If you've trained your Boxer with a clicker (see Clicker Training Basics, page 91), this is a great time to use the clicker to mark the correct behaviors.

5. **Leave frequently.** Go in and out of your front door. Go in and out of the side door. Get in the car and come back. Drive the car around the block. Vary the length of time you're gone but always leave and return without set ritual behaviors and without a big fanfare. Keep things positive, calm, and confident.

6. **Be patient.** The behaviors associated with SA weren't developed in a day, and they won't disappear in one morning. Smile. Relax. This will get better.

Extreme Separation Anxiety

This is the Boxer who starts drooling and pacing 20 minutes before you leave. He can't be crated because he becomes so panicked that he breaks teeth and pulls out toenails trying to dig, claw, and bite his way out of the crate. He may also urinate and defecate throughout the home and/or pant to the point of becoming dehydrated from being overheated.

When working with extreme cases, *consult with your veterinarian*. After ruling out possible disease-based causes for your dog's behaviors, your veterinarian may choose to prescribe one of several

2. **Use D.A.P.** Dog Appeasing Pheromone can be used as a diffuser in the room where his crate will be kept or can be sprayed lightly on his bedding.

3. **Exercise him.** A tired Boxer may be less stressed with being left alone and has a greater chance of relaxing or sleeping while you are gone.

4. **Desensitize him to departure cues.** What cues are you giving your Boxer that you are leaving? Examine these rituals and then start doing these behaviors randomly and frequently while you are home and have no intention of leaving. Pick up keys, put them back down. Lock the back door, unlock

different anti-anxiety medications *in addition* to a training program to desensitize your Boxer's separation anxiety issues. The strategies for working with a severe case of SA will include many of the same behavior modifications described for moderate or mild cases, with these *additional* caveats that will apply in the initial stages of training:

1. **Do not leave your Boxer alone.** Have a neighbor, friend, or pet sitter come in on the mornings you'll be leaving the house for work. The friend, family member, or pet sitter can distract the dog and help lessen anxiety.

2. **Take your dog somewhere new and leave him there.** If you have a doggie daycare you trust or a friend who is willing to help you with your dog, take your Boxer to this location on the mornings someone can't be with your dog at home.

3. **Do not crate your Boxer.** *Do* work on making the crate a calming, relaxing place for your Boxer.

4. **Be very patient.** It may take up to two months of concentrated effort on your part, along with possible prescription medications, to help a severe SA Boxer overcome his anxieties of being left alone.

7 *Beginning Command Training*

Now that you are working with your puppy or adult Boxer in the areas of socialization, habituation, and of course, house-training, she is well on her way to becoming a well-adjusted companion. However, if you are like most pet owners, having a semblance of control with your dog is also important, as it should be. There is nothing more well loved than the dog that is well adjusted and well mannered, and not just at home, but everywhere you go.

To achieve this "ideal" Boxer, there is some time and labor involved; however, training her is fun! Don't think of it as a chore, because it's not. If you've chosen the Boxer as your pet and companion, most likely it is because you were attracted to this breed's deep sense of devotion and the simple joy that comes from being around her. Training your dog on a regular basis gives you just one more opportunity to do something constructive and fun with her. If you approach training with the same enthusiasm and joy that

> *Do not leave a collar on your Boxer when you crate her, as it could get caught and strangle her.*

she approaches everyday living, *you will* have fun and *you will* have great success.

Equipment Essentials

Getting started with your Boxer's training requires only a few basic purchases. The following is a list of items that you will want for your Boxer and a few tips on selecting the best products for your dog.

The Collar

Flat buckle collar. Whether you own a puppy or an adult, your Boxer will need a good, solid flat buckle collar. If you begin

training her as a puppy, this may be the only collar you will need for everyday use as well as training.

Quick Release Collar. This collar has a plastic snap closure that can be easily fastened and released. It is expandable, which is great for growing puppies. Be careful not to purchase a collar with more than 2 inches of growing room, as the extra loop of material can get caught more easily and present a choking hazard.

Martingale collar. This is another collar option. The martingale collar is fashioned after the sighthound collar, which offers a

Boxers tend to get their collars caught on things a bit more often than other dogs, so be sure to take extra precautions that the collar is flat around the dog's neck, not too tight, of course, but also with no extra slack in it that can get caught or hung up on something.

broad width of collar with loops on either side through which another length of nylon runs. The collar relaxes and tightens as the dog pulls. It is broad, so that it does not choke the dog if she pulls very hard. It does tighten enough, however, that if she attempts to perform an escape move out of her collar, it simply can't be done.

Do not leave the martingale collar on your Boxer as an everyday collar in the house, as it tightens similarly to a choke collar, and if it gets caught, it can choke the dog.

Pick a Collar Just For Training. It can be the same type of collar as your dog's everyday collar—or maybe a martingale collar, if you'd like. The significance of a "special" collar used only for training is not lost on your Boxer. She will quickly recognize that the collar is linked to a training session, which of course is lots of fun. As she progresses in her training, the significance of the special collar may also mean "It's time to listen!"

Harnesses. Some owners prefer to use harnesses rather than collars on their dogs. The benefit of a harness is that pressure is never put on the dog's neck. (Veterinary chiropractors appreciate this!) If the puppy is trained at an early age not to pull, control is not an issue either, but there are some disadvantages to using a harness.

If you haven't schooled your puppy or adult, be forewarned that a harness actually allows her to pull harder and more efficiently than with a collar. (This is only true for "normal" harnesses. For information on no-pull harnesses, see page 89.) (In weight-pulling competitions, guess

TRACY'S TIPS

The prong collar has received a bad reputation, when it is actually a very useful tool when fitted correctly. The collar should be snug—not too tight but not loose—and should be fitted behind the Boxer's ears. It is a self-correcting collar, in that if the Boxer doesn't pull, the collar doesn't pinch. (The handler does not make corrections by tugging or pulling when the Boxer is wearing this collar.) Make sure that when you are fitting your Boxer for a prong collar you do not purchase the XL prongs; the prongs should not be greater than one (1) inch. This collar is only used for training and walks and is not for 24/7 wear.

what the dogs wear? Right, a harness.) Another potential downside to the harness, particularly if it is worn all the time, is that unless the harness is well-fitted and made of a nice, smooth leather, or sheepskin, it may rub your Boxer's coat and skin in some areas. Cost is also a consideration, if you have a puppy, because you will need to buy several harnesses before your Boxer has reached her full size. And finally, a harness provides more opportunities for her to get snagged on something, so it can't be left on when the Boxer is unattended or crated. Granted, if the dog's harness gets caught on a branch, she won't strangle, as she would with a snagged collar; however, if she is caught and panics, and you're not there when this happens, she can injure herself struggling and possibly even overheat or die.

The Head Halter

The head halter is a relatively new concept in training that may initially look cruel, but is actually a very gentle way for the owner to gain quick control over the dog, particularly with dogs that want to drag their owners down the street. Once you have control, you have the dog's attention. With a dog's attention, she is ready to learn.

The head halter is not to be confused with a muzzle. It is a strap that crosses over the dog's muzzle and loops behind to form a halter. The lead is snapped to a ring that is under the dog's chin.

The head halter works in a similar manner as a horse's halter: Where the head goes, the body will follow. Submissive and complacent dogs rarely put up a fuss about the head halter; however, more dominant dogs may struggle to take it off and try their best to convince you that you are being cruel. You are not! And, there are head halters designed specifically for brachycephalic breeds, such as the Boxer.

Some Boxer owners choose to put collars on their dogs only when they are with them because they fear that the opportunities for the dog to get caught and strangle herself are too great. This is true when a Boxer is in her crate; they are known to catch their collars in their crates, strangle, and die. However, leaving your Boxer without a collar at any other time is not a good idea for the following reasons:

■ A dog that bolts out the door or jumps the fence will have no visible identification. Unless someone looks for a tattoo or scans for a microchip, these alternate forms of identification may never be discovered. Both tattoo and microchip registries strongly recommend that the dog wear a tag that states, "I am tattooed," or "I am microchipped" along with the 800-number of the registry.

■ Collars and tags are often seen as a sign that the dog is a pet, and therefore friendly. A dog without a collar and perhaps one that has had some fun in the dirt is often seen as a stray and potentially dangerous, possibly frightening any would-be rescuers from touching the dog.

■ A loose dog that isn't wearing a collar is difficult to catch.

The choice of whether to keep a collar on your Boxer or not is ultimately up to you; however, with supervision and some common sense, the benefits of having your Boxer wear a collar most always outweigh the decision to go collarless. (Just ask Boxer Rescue or your local humane society!)

No-pull Harnesses

This harness works by restricting the dog's forward movement when he pulls. Several different manufacturers offer no-pull harnesses that fit and work in slightly different ways. It's best to try on different styles and sizes and have an experienced shop owner help make sure the fit is correct before you make a purchase.

The Leash

In addition to a collar, you will also need to purchase a training leash. For puppies, make sure you purchase the lightest, thinnest leash you can, approximately 6 feet (1.8 m) in length. Yes, you will need to purchase a much sturdier leash when your pup is a bit bigger; however, a large leash now would mean your precious puppy's head would be constantly smacked with a big heavy buckle. So invest in a lightweight leash initially, and then purchase a heavier leash when your puppy is a bit bigger. (You might find yourself using the lighter leash with a well-trained adult, however, so don't throw it away!)

If you own an adult Boxer, you can purchase whatever leash you'd like. If your dog pulls a lot, you may consider a leather leash or one made of a cotton web fabric that won't chafe your hands. Nylon is very sturdy, but it can be tough to hold with an untrained and boisterous Boxer. Avoid purchasing any chain link leashes; these products are difficult to hold, cumbersome, and they portray the wrong image for both you and your dog. Also, do not use a retractable leash for training. This doesn't give you the close working control you'll need initially. And, if you forget to lock the leash, once your Boxer goes running out, it's nearly impossible to reel him back in!

Reinforcements

We've talked about positive reinforcements briefly in a previous chapter (see Positive Reinforcement, page 17), but now is the time to think about what type of reinforcement is easiest for you to work with and to which your Boxer responds well.

Food

Used as rewards and lures, food treats are probably the most popular form of reinforcement being used nationwide in training schools. "Treating" a dog is one way to promote positive, gentle training. Food has many benefits as a training tool. It's easy to lure a dog into a position with food for such commands as "*Sit*," and "*Down*," and for various tricks. If used before meals when the dog is hungry, the Boxer is usually motivated to earn his treats. A third benefit, and one of particular interest to owners of deaf Boxers, is that using the treat to position the dog into the command allows the other hand to be free to give the dog a hand signal.

A drawback to the food reward system is that it's simply not a motivator for some Boxers. In particular, dogs that are a bit uncomfortable or uneasy in their surroundings may refuse food. On the other hand, there are some dogs that will do anything for a treat, and when rewarded frequently, gain weight. This can be

Healthy Treat Options

When considering what foods to use as rewards, the treat must be regarded as something particularly desirable by the dog, and it must be healthy. Look for treats that are low or devoid of salts and low in sugars and fats, as they can cause digestive upset. Healthy choices include:

- Natural, prepackaged training treats. Several manufacturers are making all-natural training treats with healthy ingredients and without preservatives. These treats are available in both chewy or baked forms that can be broken into very, very small pieces. (Tiny baked training treats are less messy in pockets and don't require a training treat bag to be worn when working with your Boxer.)
- Home-cooked tidbits. Baked chicken breasts with garlic, liver (grilled outdoors so as not to

stink up the kitchen), and microwaved, low-sodium healthy hot dogs can all be chopped into very small pieces and used as treats.
- Raw vegetables. Some dogs love carrots. Chop these into small bits and use as rewards.
- Dry dog food. Highly food-motivated dogs may work for a portion of their daily meals. Additionally, if you are working throughout the day with your Boxer (i.e., your Boxer is working on a lot of behaviors at the same time), you can portion your Boxer's entire daily rations as training treats.

countered, however, by figuring the food rewards into your puppy's or adult dog's total daily food allowances.

Praise

Boxers can never get too much lovin', and that includes verbal and physical praise. Dogs immediately recognize happiness in our voices, and they also thoroughly

enjoy being touched, rubbed, and patted. The effectiveness of praise has been well documented, and is something that should be used when training your Boxer. Verbal and physical praise can be used in conjunction with another reward system such as a treat or toy, or on its own. The advantages to using praise also include that it can be "faded" successfully. In other words, it is easy to transition from praising your dog verbally and physically every time she sits on command, to praising your dog verbally every time and physically every so often, to finally praising your dog only at the end of a series of successful commands. A drawback to using praise alone in your training is that there is no way to "lure" your dog into position for certain commands.

Toys

Some Boxers are crazy about balls. If you own a ball-crazed Boxer, you may very well want to use a tennis ball on a rope for your reward system. Padded, sausage-like tug toys on a rope can also be used very successfully in training. Though luring a dog into position with a toy can be cumbersome, working with the toy as a reward can be very successful.

When using the toy as a reward, keep the toy out of sight or in your right hand, depending on the exercise you are working on. When the dog completes the command or exercise, reward her by allowing her to grab and play with the toy. Balls and toys on a rope work well because you can hold one end of the toy at all times. When the reward/play is over, you can then give the *out* command (see *Out*, page 113), and take back the toy.

Clicker Training

Clicker training conditions the dog to accept a "click" from a clicker as a verbal reward and a promise of a treat. Initially, the treat comes with every click; this is how the dog learns to associate a click with a

treat. Then the treats are faded so that the dog still gets treated when she has received clicks, but the treat may not come until the dog has received several clicks.

The main advantages to clicker training are in the method's precision, and the ability to reward the dog at a distance by sound. The precision of a click is much more exact than trying to say "*Good, girl*!" or treating a dog. With verbal praise, the timing is approximate to when the dog performs the task. With treats, the dog typically doesn't get rewarded until sometime after she has performed the task. With the clicker, the dog knows she is being rewarded the moment she performs the task successfully.

As for distance training, clicker training works well to reward your Boxer and reinforce a behavior when your dog is out of reach. For example, if you are training your dog to jump though a hoop, with

clicker training you can now "click" and thereby reward your dog while she is airborne going through the hoop!

The only disadvantage to this system (and it is a very minor disadvantage!) is that the owner needs to have a certain level of coordination to be able to handle the dog, treats, and clicker. Don't worry. With a little practice, you'll get it! (<click>, treat, "Good girl!") To learn more about clicker training, see Useful Addresses and Literature, page 160.

Selecting a Trainer and Training School

Training your Boxer is easier with the help of someone who has "been there/done that" and loves training new owners with their dogs. Books and training videos are exceptionally helpful and are great references, but nothing ever really replaces hands-on training *with a terrific instructor*—particularly if you're having difficulties training your Boxer.

So how do you find a training class? One of the best ways is to simply ask. Ask your veterinarian what school he or she recommends. Ask the local humane society for a recommendation. If you're fortunate enough to live in the same area as your breeder, be sure to ask him or her for a recommendation. Do you have any neighbors who have well-trained dogs that you admire? Ask them where they went for training.

You'll quickly find that one or two training clubs are mentioned frequently. When you're at this point, call the school and talk to them about the class, what types of things are taught (it should be a mixture of command work along with socialization—for puppies—and troubleshooting typical problem behaviors), and what type of experience and accreditations or certifications the trainer has. If this goes well, your next step is to arrange to visit a class—without your Boxer— while it is in session.

When you're at the school, you'll want to watch for several things.

■ Is the training facility clean? When training young puppies it is critical that the floors are kept clean to prevent infection. Remember that puppies that begin training are usually in the middle of their vaccination series, and therefore are still susceptible to a variety of diseases. Even if you are training an adult dog, cleanliness counts. Health dangers still lurk in dirty surroundings.

■ What is the tone of the class? Training should be *fun*. If the trainer is heavy-handed and not fun you'll pick this up quickly by the way the students in the class are participating.

- Does the trainer inspire you? A great trainer combines skill, experience, and enthusiasm and freely shares all of this with his or her students. A trainer who is lacking in any or all of these areas is not a good choice.

    Hint: If you're not comfortable with the trainer, no matter how awesome his or her reputation, you're not going to listen as well or benefit much from the trainer's experience.

- Does the trainer teach using the tools and reinforcements you want to use? If you're interested in clicker training, make sure you find a trainer comfortable with this method of training. If you'd like to work with a head halter, make sure the trainer is skilled in training with this tool.
- Do you see any slip or choke collars? If you are watching a puppy class and you see choke collars being used, find another class. Young puppies as a general rule never need this type of correction. If you're watching an adult

training class and you see slip collars, you may want to ask the trainer why these collars are being used.

- Does the trainer like Boxers? As hard as this may be to fathom, there are trainers who will groan and roll their eyes if they hear someone wants to train a Boxer. What this tells you is that the trainer is inexperienced working with this breed and you should find another trainer. Someone who has worked with Boxers and is skilled with them will be delighted to have the opportunity to work with such a wonderful creature!

If you like what you see and you enjoy the trainer, then sign up. Many schools fill their early puppy classes in a hurry, so if this happens to be the situation, don't despair. Sign up for the earliest available class and make sure to get your name on the waiting list of any other classes that precede it. Owners often sign up for classes but never attend or drop out quickly. Sometimes this can mean a space may open up. It's worth a try.

If it will be a few weeks before you can get into a class, this doesn't mean you can take time off until class time! With a young puppy it is important to begin training right away, and with the guidelines in this book, you can have your puppy responding solidly to several commands within a few weeks.

If you're working with an adult Boxer, the chances are much greater that you will find an open class, but if you can't, there's no reason to wait to train your dog either. Start at home, keep it positive, and have fun, because, isn't F-U-N how you spell "Boxer"?

TRACY'S TIPS

The Boxer is not a prepackaged, trained dog. You have to invest a substantial amount of time into training your Boxer so that she can reach her full potential as a loving, social, well-trained companion that you will feel comfortable taking with you everywhere.

Home Schooling

The "Five Ws" of Training

To make the most of your training sessions with your Boxer, there are a few basics of training that can make your job *much* simpler. The "Five Ws" of training are as follows.

Who

The "who" of training is, of course, you and your Boxer. It is important that you are in a good mood during the training. If you are having a bad day and are running on a short fuse, this is not the time to attempt to work on training your dog. She will read you like a book and attempt to "please" you (i.e., make you happy), but not necessarily by learning and obeying your commands. So make sure that you are as enthusiastic as she is going into your training sessions. Remember: Patience really is a virtue when it comes to training.

What

Proper training equipment for both handler and Boxer is important. You should be sure to wear athletic shoes for good grip and traction. Loose floppy shoes are difficult to move well in and are also a distraction to a playful Boxer—a new chew toy! The training essentials for your dog have already been covered in this chapter but include a good collar, leash, and treats or other rewards.

Where

Aside from your weekly group training sessions with a trainer, your daily sessions should be in areas with very few distractions so that your Boxer can really focus on you. In the beginning, you're really trying to maximize the potential for her to do the right thing: You're not trying to test her at this point. So don't try to teach her the *sit* in the kitchen if someone is cooking dinner on the stove, or in the backyard if you have children or other pets running around. Try to keep your daily sessions in a quiet place with few distractions. As she becomes more proficient in her command work, then you will want to begin working in areas with more and more distractions.

When

When you are just starting out training your Boxer, whether you own an adult or a puppy, she will need many successful repetitions of a task to learn the behavior you want her to perform. What this means is that the more mini-sessions you can have throughout the day and evening, the faster she will learn because you are constantly reinforcing her correct response to the command. If you don't have the ben-

efit of being home all day to work off and on with your Boxer, the next best method is to schedule two or three short sessions of five minutes or so, spread out in a day.

Shorter training sessions also help to keep her from becoming bored and adding new twists to the exercises being taught. A Boxer, as mentioned earlier, likes to keep life interesting and this extends to her training. Keep the training sessions interesting and playful, and always stop before she tires either mentally or physically. Timing is important!

Why

The importance of a well-trained Boxer has already been discussed in this chapter, but in summary, it is important to train her to be a good canine for several reasons:

- A well-behaved dog is a joy to live with.
- A well-trained dog is less of a liability in this lawsuit-happy world.
- Every minute you put into training your dog deepens the bond you have with her—and isn't that what dog ownership is all about?

8 *Seven Basic Commands*

You and your Boxer can potentially "get by" knowing very few commands. Depending on your lifestyle and what you expect from him, the basic seven skills—Name, Collar touch, *Sit*, *Stay*, *Down*, *Come*, and *Walk nicely*—can be quite sufficient for most pet owners.

What many dog owners discover though, is that they enjoy teaching their dogs new commands and tricks. So whether you read past this chapter to pick up additional home-living skills to teach your Boxer, or if you simply stop with the "basic seven," it is really up to you and your family's needs. Regardless of how far you take your Boxer, teaching a few (or a lot) of commands will help to shape a controllable and fun pet.

Name

Though people often don't think of their dogs' names as a "command" as such, it is an important foundation skill. First, you want your dog to recognize his name. Your Boxer puppy will come with a registered name and the breeder may have given him a nickname; however, you may want to change his "call" name to something you feel is more appropriate to his personality, coloring, or markings. Teaching the puppy his new name is important!

Or, perhaps you've adopted an adult dog. The dog may have had a name, which you may want to change, or the Boxer's name may be unknown and you need to *give* him a name. Teaching the rescued Boxer his name is a vital first step, too.

But this isn't the most important reason behind teaching a dog his name. You want to go a step farther and teach your Boxer that his name means that he is to respond by giving you his full and undivided attention. In this way, the Boxer's name becomes a "set-up" for what's coming next—a command. If your Boxer is listening and attentive, he is going to hear and respond to your commands.

Teaching the Name

1. Say your Boxer's name when he is looking directly at you.
2. Reward him with praise and a treat.
3. Repeat whenever you catch your Boxer looking at you.
4. As your Boxer connects his name with looking at you, say his name when he is close to you and not distracted.
5. When he turns an eye to look at you, praise and reward!
6. Practice and reward for eye turns.
7. Increase the ante: now you want a full head turn before he gets praise and rewards.

Keep practicing saying your Boxer's name and keep it fun. You want him to love hearing his name. Gradually increase what your Boxer needs to do to receive praise and reward for hearing his name until you have him doing a full body turn (even when headed the other direction). Your ultimate goal is for your Boxer to

hear his name and come running to you *without being given the* Come *command.*

Collar Touch

This isn't a command, as such, but it is an important conditioning exercise for Boxers of all ages. Often "collaring," grabbing or lunging to grab a wayward Boxer's collar, is seen as an aggressive move, which can be frightening to him—or in the case of a very confident Boxer, an attempt to grab his collar could be the beginning of the best game of keep-away ever.

You will never win a game of keep-a-way with a Boxer . . . and a frightened puppy that won't allow strangers to grasp his collar will likewise never be caught if he is loose and lost.

Fortunately, the *collar touch* is very simple to teach.

1. When your Boxer is getting pats from you, gently touch his collar.
2. Release and reward him with praise and a treat.
3. Continue praising and reward him every time he allows you to touch his collar without bolting or exhibiting stressed or fearful behaviors. He should be calm and relaxed.
4. When he is comfortable with you touching his collar, begin grasping his collar briefly.
5. Reward and praise calm, happy behaviors.
6. Continue practicing and rewarding good behaviors until he associates someone grasping his collar (and restraining him, if necessary) as a good thing.

Sit

If your Boxer learns only one command, this is it: the *sit*. The *sit* command comes in handy for so many things in everyday life that it is virtually indispensable.

■ If your Boxer tends to want to jump and hug every person on earth, a *sit* command can keep him on the ground.
■ When it's feeding time, a *sit* command keeps the dinner bowl from being knocked to the floor.
■ A *sit* can be used to keep your Boxer from rushing through open doors ahead of you.
■ It can also be used as a "defusing" command. If he is behaving badly or simply is too wound up, you can put him on a *sit*, and then reward him for this "good" behavior.
■ A solid *sit* command has also been used more than once to catch a loose Boxer or to break up play that is going over the top.

So, without anything more said, the *sit* command is very valuable, and who knows how many ways you will be able to use this command. The more you practice

TRACY'S TIPS

Verbal commands should always be "business-like calm." Not a begging tone and not too harsh. If the command is harsh, the Boxer thinks he is in trouble and then the command becomes a bad word, making the Boxer more on edge.

Release Commands: *Many people will automatically begin giving their dogs what is called a release command after the dog has performed a task; however, it is important that the word used to release your dog from a command is the same every time. Many owners choose to use "O.K." or "Yes!" which are both fine choices. The release should be a single word—your Boxer won't focus in on longer phrases—and it should be something that you use naturally when your Boxer has done something great.*

it at home and around the neighborhood, the faster and more consistently your Boxer will respond.

Teaching the Sit

1. With your hand gently holding your dog's collar, say his name.
2. Hold a treat in the palm of your right hand with your fingers wrapped around it.
3. When you have achieved eye contact, begin passing the hand with the treat directly in front of your dog's nose slowly over the top of his head to about the back of the skull. Your hand should be so close to the top of your dog's head as to almost brush the hairs. What should happen is that he will follow the treat with his nose and as you move it farther back, he will automatically sit.

4. The moment he folds into a *sit*, say "*Sit!*" Do not say the word *sit* or anything else until he is actually in the final act of sitting with no chance of not completing the *sit* (see Word and Signal Association, page 21).

5. If you fail to get your Boxer to sit on your first try, don't give up! Try again, making sure not to allow him to back up while the treat is passing over his head. This will force him to tuck in his rear end, rock back, and sit.

6. Once you have him sitting, give him his well-earned treat, enthusiastically give your release word (see Release Commands, page 99) and give lots of pats and praise!

Hand Signals

Once you have your Boxer sitting without having to pass the food over his head to shape the *sit*, you can begin adding a hand signal.

1. Holding the treat in your right hand, say his name.

2. When you have his attention (which should be immediate now), raise your left hand and, while giving the hand signal of your choice, say "*Sit.*" For hand

signals, you may use a touch to the chin, a sweep upward with an open palm, the American Sign Language symbol for *sit*, or a hand signal that you choose that is specific to a certain performance event. Whatever you choose, make sure you are consistent and make the same hand gesture every time you say *"Sit."*

3. Release, praise, and treat, of course!
4. As your Boxer begins sitting regularly on command, begin fading the verbal cue, saying *"Sit"* only sometimes while giving the hand signal. If your dog doesn't respond immediately, refrain from giving the command again; instead, shape your Boxer into a sit with a treat while giving the hand signal.
5. Practice, practice, practice!

Stay

If *sit* is a good command to know, then *sitting* and *staying* are even better! The *stay* command is another very practical command for your Boxer to learn, and it may even save his life someday. The *stay* command comes in handy when clipping his toenails, giving him baths, grooming him, and preventing him from bolting out the front door, as well as preventing a loose Boxer from getting hit by a car.

The *stay* command is a relatively easy task to teach your Boxer; however, it is important to note that you should never "test" your dog off leash on the *stay* command in an unfenced area, just in case the motivators you are using (praise, treats, toys, etc.) aren't quite as motivating as the dog next door or the child walking by with an ice cream cone.

Teaching the Stay Command

1. Get your dog's attention by saying his name.
2. With him at your left side, put him into a *sit*.
3. Holding the leash in your right hand, say *"Stay"* while, with your left hand, give the hand signal for *stay* directly in front of his nose. The hand signal is generally a flat hand, palm facing toward the dog, fingers pointing toward the ground.
4. Do not move! Remain in this position for a few seconds, then reward him with a release command and a treat.
5. Add movement. As your Boxer understands that *"Stay"* means *"don't move,"* add a step-away. Put your Boxer in a *sit-stay*, and take a small step sidewise to the right with your right foot while keeping your left foot in place. Step immediately back. Praise. Release. Repeat.
6. Add time. Repeat number 5 above, but this time rock your weight onto the right foot and hold this position for 3 seconds. Rock back and step back with the right foot. Praise. Release. Repeat.
7. Add distance. Repeat #5 but this time bring your left together with your right foot so you are one complete sidestep away from your Boxer. Immediately step back. Praise. Release. Repeat.
8. Add time, again. See how this works? Increase only one variable at a time. When your Boxer is solid with #7, add 3 seconds to the stay. Praise. Release. Repeat.

9. Add a new direction. Stepping forward is hard with the *stay* and why learning not to move when you step to the side is initially easier for your Boxer. When you add a step forward, your Boxer's natural instincts are to follow you. Help your Boxer by giving the *sit-stay* command and taking a small step forward with the **right** foot and then immediately step back. (Stepping forward on the left foot is reserved for a quick, snappy motion response from your Boxer to follow you.) Praise. Release. Repeat.

10. Continue to work on increased time and distance, as well as different directions—but not all at the same time. If your Boxer seems confused at any time, take a step back (often literally) and make the exercise easier with either less time on the *stay*, an easier direction, or less distance. Work back up to more difficult *sit-stays* gradually. As your Boxer becomes more proficient with the *stay* command, you can increase the amount of time that he must sit next to you by a minute.

Be sure not to push your Boxer too soon. It's better to go a bit slower and make sure he has learned the *sit-stay* than to rush to more advanced levels of the *stay*, fail (the dog breaks the *stay*), and have to retrace your steps. Continue to build on the *sit-stay* by increasing one variable at a time until you can walk the distance of a 6 foot leash in any direction and your Boxer will remain in this position for several minutes.

To the Test?

Unless you are planning to enter a competitive sport with your dog, it is advisable *never* to test your dog's abilities to follow your commands off leash in an unfenced area. Why? Because without the ability to enforce the command, such as a leash to catch your dog before he runs off, your Boxer's learning is inconsistent.

On the reality side of things: Even if you are sure that your Boxer is steady on his *sit-stay* command, the one time you try this off leash in an open area is the one time it is virtually guaranteed that a squirrel or rabbit will run right under his nose. Now you have a loose dog that is far more motivated by the running critter than the treat in your hand. You also have a Boxer that has learned maybe he doesn't have to do everything you ask him to.

A mistake that many new owners make when working their dogs is to repeat commands. This is a no-no because if you repeat the command several times before the dog responds, you're actually teaching your dog to be slow and wait for several commands.

So what do you do if your dog doesn't respond the first time to a command? When he really knows his commands well and doesn't respond, it is often because you don't have his attention. So, make sure you have his attention before giving any commands; you want to set your Boxer up for success, not try to test his learning ability. Then, if you have the dog's attention and he doesn't perform the command, help him. Take him back to square one and lure him into position using a treat. Rebuild his response to the command being careful not to go too fast with him.

If you are training for Agility, competitive obedience, Schutzhund obedience, or other dog sports, you will eventually need to work with your dog off leash as part of your training and testing, but this work is still performed in protected, fenced-in areas.

The real test of what your dog has learned is, of course, in the emergency situation when you *really* need your dog to *sit*, *stay*, or *come*. Hopefully, you won't have to be confronted with this type of situation, but if you are—and you've really worked hard with your Boxer—the odds are in your favor that he will indeed listen to you and obey your command willingly.

Down

The *down* command is a very useful tool in everyday Boxer life. The *down* can be used as a settling tool. If a Boxer has a temporary case of the rowdies, he can be put in a *down* to help calm him. If he is barking at something, you can add distance by walking away from the stimulus and then put him in a *down* to discourage his barking. (It's difficult for a dog to bark in a *down*.)

The *down* also can be used to gently reinforce leadership by all family members, big and small. The *down* is a submissive position, and by asking your Boxer to *down*, you are kindly establishing and/or reinforcing or maintaining a leadership role.

Teaching the Down

1. With your Boxer at your left side (and on leash) put her in a *sit*.
2. Holding a treat in one hand, move the treat from right in front of his nose slowly down to the floor while saying the command *"Down."* In a perfect world, he should follow the treat to the floor and wind up lying down.
3. This is not a perfect world. Your Boxer is likely to go rump up and front end down to reach the treat. Keep trying. It's okay to give him the treat

people will say "*Get down*" when they want their dogs to hop off a couch or, "*Down*", when the Boxer jumps up on a person. Don't confuse your Boxer! Instead, use the *off* command (see *Off*, page 111) for those times when you want your Boxer to get off a chair, couch, bed, or you!

Teaching the Down-Stay

Once your Boxer has mastered the *down*, you can begin working on the *down-stay*. This is done in much the same way that the *sit-stay* is taught (See *Sit*, pages 99–101.)

1. Put your Boxer in a *down*.
2. Bend over and give him the *stay* hand signal with your left hand (fingers down, palm toward the front of his nose, and a right-to-left motion).
3. If your Boxer understands the word "stay," walk a step away with your *right* foot. Come back to him. If he doesn't know what "stay" means, don't walk away from him; stand still next to him for a few seconds.
4. Release, praise, and treat!
5. As your dog gets steadier in staying with this command, you can walk farther away until you are at the end of the leash. To practice this at an even greater distance, use a recall leash. Eventually, a puppy should be able to *down-stay* for several minutes at a time. (Adult Boxers will be able to *down-stay* for much longer periods.)
6. If you need a refresher on how to progress using time and distance with the *down-stay*, see tips given for the *sit-stay* on page 101.

as he makes the effort to lie down. This is part of the "shaping" method described on page 18. Do not, however, utter the word "*down*" until the Boxer is completely in a full *down* with elbows, chest, and haunches completely (and without question) on the ground. In fact, don't start linking the voice command for *down* with the full *down* until you are able to consistently lure your Boxer into the actual position.

4. When he is lying down, and only then, say "*Down*!" Reward him with the treat.
5. Give him the release word, praise, and a pat!
6. Be sure when working with this command that your dog realizes he cannot break the *down* until you give the release command.

Did You Mean Down?

A problem that often crops up with the *down* command is that the handler uses this command for an action other than the *down* and confuses the dog. Frequently,

Come

The *recall* exercise, as it is called in formal obedience, is not only practical, but it may just be what saves your wayward Boxer's life some day. The *come* command is not difficult to teach with either puppies or adults. As with any exercise, this command should not be taught off leash. If you are planning to participate in obedience trials, you will have to recall your dog off leash; however, this exercise should only be practiced off leash if he is very solid in his on-leash *recall*, and you are in a fenced protected area.

There are many, many ways to teach the *come* command. The underlying principle of all these exercises is to make it so much fun for the Boxer to run to you that he can hardly contain himself!

The following are a few favorites that involve all family members.

Teaching the Come

1. In a room in the house or in a fenced backyard, have family members sit in a circle.
2. With a lightweight leash on the dog, have one family member hold him gently.
3. Have another family member (only one!) say the Boxer's name (this is to get his attention), and then do whatever it takes to entice the Boxer to come running to him or her.
4. When the puppy is nearly in the arms of the family member who is calling him, have that person say "*Come*!" The goal is to give the command when you

Be Careful!

When teaching the come, be careful to never punish your boxer for coming to you. This sounds crazy ("Why would I punish my dog for coming to me?"), but it happens quite often and quite accidently. For example, if your Boxer is shredding your slipper, do you call him over to you and then chew him out for chewing up the slipper? He sees this as being punished for coming to you. Or, maybe your Boxer puppy escaped from the front door and has played catch-me-if-you-can (which you can't) and you've spent a good half-hour calling him. When he finally comes, do you scold him for playing hard to catch? He interprets this as being punished for coming to you, too.

It's easy to do and almost everyone finds themselves in this position. No matter how irritated you are with your Boxer, always praise him for coming to you—even if it's with a slobbery half slipper in his mouth or after he's had you chasing him in the yard. He came. He gets rewarded. Next time, he will come even faster! That's your reward for not punishing him.

are 99 percent sure the dog will actually complete the *come*.

5. When he comes running, do not lunge or grab for the collar (this can start him

on a perpetual game of keep-away), but catch the leash. Praise profusely and treat!

6. Once the Boxer has received his treat, have another family member call him and continue the exercise.

Note: Be sure not to go too long with this exercise. You want your Boxer joyful and eager to come running to you. Be sure to quit the game while he wants more.

Alternative method. Of course, not everyone has a full family at their disposal to play the *come* game. If you are on your

> **TRACY'S TIPS**
> *The recall is perhaps the most important command you can teach your Boxer. It's a lifesaving command. Make sure it's fun when you are teaching it to your Boxer, and make sure you train this skill!*

> **TRACY'S TIPS**
> *Use dinner for the come command. Bang the dinner dish, and when your Boxer comes running in for his dinner, give the come command. His reward is lots of praise—and his dinner!*

own, however, there are still some fun exercises you can do to help teach your Boxer that "come" does indeed mean "*come.*"

1. Give the *come* command whenever your Boxer is running toward you, but only when you are virtually positive he is coming to you. Encourage him to come even faster with your body language (be relaxed, loose, and having fun!) and voice ("*Faster!*" "*Let's go!*" "*Woohoo!*"). As simple as this sounds, if you are consistent in giving the command—and it should be in a joyful

To really put speed and dazzle on your recall, Norbert Zawatzki, Director of Training for the German Boxer Club, recommends tossing a ball through your legs and behind you just as your Boxer approaches you. He will come zooming through your legs and snatch up the ball behind you. The tossed ball not only motivates him to run hard on his recall, it is also his immediate reward for coming so quickly, and a great way to keep training fun.

and excited manner (who would want to come running to a surly owner?)—your Boxer will quickly connect that running to you means good things.

2. Encourage an even faster recall by turning your back to your Boxer when he is just two or three strides away and running *away from him as fast as you can*. He will really get excited! And don't worry, he'll catch you.

3. Praise your Boxer lavishly for coming, and reward with a toy or a treat and lots of attention, of course!

Note: This manner of teaching the *come* command can work well if your dog knows you have a sack of treats with you, and it's before suppertime.

On-leash Come

Once your Boxer has figured out that "*come*" means to come running, you can work on the exercise in combination with a *sit-stay* while on a leash. The benefit to using the *sit-stay* and a leash for this intermediate level of the *recall* is that you can now work on this exercise in a variety of locations, not just your fenced backyard or a room in your home. The more your Boxer is accustomed to coming when you call him, in all sorts of surroundings, the more likely he will come when you really need him to.

1. Put your Boxer in a *sit-stay* and walk to the end of the leash.

2. Say his name to get his attention.

3. Give the *come* command and start jogging a bit backwards while enthusiastically encouraging him to come running, but being careful not to repeat the *come* command.

4. When he catches up with you, praise him lavishly and give him some treats.

5. If you are planning to compete in obedience at some point, you will eventually want to add a *sit* in front of you and a *finish to heel* position. This isn't necessary now, however, because you want that unbridled enthusiasm of a Boxer streaking toward you!
6. The *recall* can be performed at increasingly longer distances using a tracking leash or retractable leash.

Involving the Kids

If you have children, training your Boxer to listen to their commands is as important as training him to listen to your commands. As a family dog that likes to be involved in *everything*, if your Boxer listens to your children, group playtimes can become even more fun. Also, children tend to be avid learners when it comes to dog training and will (generally) readily accept your instructions.

First, make sure your Boxer is steady in responding to a command before you attempt to have your children learn to give him the same command. A good first command to teach is the *sit*. Have your child stand next to you, facing your dog, and give your dog the command "*Sit.*" (If your child is small, sit down and put your child in your lap.) When the Boxer sits, have your child reward him with a treat. Release the dog ("*O.K!*") and then have your child give him the same *sit* command, and reward as soon as he sits.

Tip: If you have young children (5 to 13), you might consider teaching hand signals to them and your Boxer for the commands. A child's high-pitched voice

lacks the authority of an adult, but a hand signal "reads" the same. Also, make sure your children know not to try to "train" the dog while you are not there. They could very quickly confuse the dog or train him to do something you don't want him to do!

Walk Nicely

If there's one common complaint about the Boxer, it is that this breed, when not trained, has a fond tendency of dragging his hapless owner on walks. Motivators, such as treats, praise, and balls, can work—but only to a certain point. Why? Because when you are out on a walk, there are generally so many fascinating things that your Boxer just can't wait to explore. You have a treat in your hand? Huh. That's nothing compared to that puppy across the street or the bird that just flew up in that tree or that leaf falling from a bush or—you get the point.

Walking nicely on a leash can be difficult to train for many owners mainly because Boxers have such a great interest in their surroundings coupled with a virtually endless supply of energy; however, there are quite a few training techniques and tools available that can make this job simpler.

Training the Walk Nicely

1. Allow your Boxer to burn off a little energy (if possible) in the backyard with a game of chase or some ball throwing.

2. Attach a 6-foot (1.8-m) leash with a suitable clip (small for little puppies, large is fine for adults).
3. Carry (and make sure your Boxer *knows* you are carrying) a motivator such as treats or a favorite tug toy.
4. Begin walking. If you are planning on competing in obedience at some point, be sure to begin with your *left* foot, leaning into the first step for a body cue. This left step will later signal your dog to move with you as opposed to staying in place, which will be indicated by leading off with your *right* foot.
5. Use your voice and lots of praise, as well as occasional treats to keep your Boxer's attention focused on you.
6. To keep his attention, try mixing things up. If he goes one way, you go the other. If he lunges ahead, do an about-turn and being walking the other way. If he veers left, turn to the right quickly. If he lags, speed up and encourage him to catch up. Keep changing directions until he realizes he must pay attention or he will be left behind.
7. If you are carrying a tug toy or a ball on a rope, carry this in your right hand (your Boxer is on your left) and swing your right arm so that he catches glimpses of the toy, recommends Zawatzki. Occasionally let your Boxer have the toy and play a short game as a reward. (This works wonders with adult Boxers, too.)

Problem Pullers

If a Boxer is not walked frequently as a puppy, problems can occur when the dog matures or is later adopted as an adult dog. For heavy pullers or adult dogs that just can't seem to pay attention to *you*, look into investing in a head collar (see The Head Halter, page 88) or a no-pull harness, or for heavy pullers a prong collar (see pages 63 and 87). You can use these tools while working on good leash manners. If your Boxer pulls and lunges and barks at other dogs, see pages 62–66 for tips on overcoming leash aggression.

9 *Seven More Commands*

Ready to learn some additional commands for your Boxer? With the basics in Chapter 8, you should be well on your way to having a great house dog, but these additional commands will give you some additional control. Choose those that are most needed for your lifestyle and work on them a few times for short periods throughout the day.

Off

This is the command that is used to get your Boxer off the couch, off the bed, or off any other piece of furniture she shouldn't be on. Using the *off* command enables the Boxer owner to instill gentle leadership skills and refrain from ever having to use force to require a Boxer to vacate a "people" space. As mentioned in teaching the *down* command, be sure not to use the word "down" for this command because it only creates confusion.

Teaching the Off

1. Say your Boxer's name to get her attention.
2. Coax her off the furniture or bed with a treat or a toy, saying the command *"Off."*
3. Praise her and take her to another room or area.

4. If you'd like, you can add a hand signal (a sweeping motion works well) when you say the command *"Off."*

Stand

Teaching your Boxer to stand still on all four feet may seem like an impossibility, particularly if you have a Boxer that prefers to be airborne; however, this simple command is crucial for everyday grooming procedures. It also is a command that your veterinarian will greatly appreciate during yearly examinations! If you are considering competitive obedience or perhaps showing your Boxer in the conformation ring, the *stand* is something you will need to teach her, too.

Teaching the Stand

1. With your Boxer on leash and at your left side, take a couple of steps forward, pull back slightly to halt her. As she is standing—here's the part that requires a bit of coordination—put your left hand, fingers down, in front of her nose and say *"Stand."*
2. If your Boxer tries to sit, quickly scoop her up by putting your hand under her abdomen area.
3. Release her when she is standing still.
4. Praise and treat her.

Teaching the Stand-Stay

The second part of this command is the *stay* portion. (Note: She should know the concept of the *sit-stay* first.) To teach this to your dog, follow these steps.

1. In the *stand* position, give your Boxer the *stay* hand signal (a quick right to left, fingers down movement).
2. Holding the leash in your right hand, stay in this position for a few seconds and then release her. Praise and treat!
3. Gradually increase the time you ask your Boxer to stand without moving. (If she moves a foot, say "*Ah!*" and move the foot back into position.)
4. Add distance to the *stand-stay*. Take a step away to the side and back. Release and praise.

5. Follow the principles of adding either time or distance—but not both at the same time—to make the *stand-stay* more difficult. (Refer to the *sit-stay*, page 101, for guidelines on how to add variables to an exercise.)
6. As she progresses, you will eventually be able to walk away from her in varying distances. Be sure to always keep a leash on her so that you can control your dog if she should break her *stand-stay*.

Take It *and* Out

The Boxer's bite is made for holding onto things and not letting go. So if you plan on playing tug with her, or if you are to have any hope of retrieving a wayward shoe from her jaws, you'll need to teach her the *out* command.

Of course, going hand-in-hand with the *out* command is the *take it* command, and the two can be taught simultaneously.

Teaching the Take It

1. Choose a toy that your Boxer really, really wants to take in her mouth and play with. For some dogs this might be a favorite ball or a stuffed dog toy. (Food items, such as meaty bones, should be avoided. Though your Boxer will gladly take it, there could be some issues with resource guarding that could make the "out" part of the exercise unnecessarily difficult. For guidelines on working with resource guarding, see pages 132–135.)

But That's a Bribe!
Yup. It is! But it works and it's non-confrontational. Why is it important to entice your dog to do something rather than force her? If—by chance—a dog has taken a dominant role and sees her position as elevated (sitting on a couch or lying on her master's bed can be viewed by a dog as "elevated" or giving her a higher status in the family) and a person physically tries to force the Boxer from this position, this force can be met with a threatening growl, a snarl, or even a snap or bite. There is no reason to force the issue and thereby give your Boxer an opportunity to fail.

Always keep it positive. And guess what? You will have won in the end anyway. By luring your Boxer off the couch or bed and teaching her a solid off command, you will work toward establishing and maintaining leadership from you.

as some of the fun toys your Boxer can "take" and play with. (Don't let her play with them unsupervised.) This is a technique commonly seen in Germany that incorporates retrieving items into the assortment of play items. It works! If your Boxer sees the dumbbell as something fun to pick up, you will rarely have a problem with retrieves later.

Teaching the Out

Whether you like playing tug with your Boxer or simply want your Boxer to drop something he's not supposed to have (like a shoe, sock, or stick), you'll want to be able to give the *out* command and have your Boxer drop the item (or give back the tug).

2. Standing in front of your Boxer, put her in a *sit*.
3. Hold the toy near her mouth (so she doesn't have to break the *sit* to get it)
4. When she opens her mouth and takes the toy, say "*Take it!*"
5. Immediately give her a release command (so she can break the *sit*) and play a little tug with her or let her run around shaking her prize.
6. If you are considering competitive obedience, be sure to include dumbbells

The trick in teaching the *out* is to use a reward that is valued higher by the Boxer than the item she is holding in her mouth. Treats or high reward items such as garlic chicken can be used for this exercise.

1. With the dog under control (hand on the collar or dog on leash), say her name and give her the *sit* command. (This gets her attention and alerts her that playtime is over.)
2. Offer her the highly coveted reward.
3. As she drops the item from her mouth, say "*Out!*"
4. Praise her and give her a treat. Repetition works wonders and your Boxer will quickly learn that releasing the item means a treat.

Leave It

This command is closely related to the *out* command, except you never allow the dog to pick up the article or item. This command can be practiced frequently on walks when you want your Boxer not to touch or sniff something, such as a dead bird.

Teaching the Leave It

1. While walking your Boxer on a leash, keep an eye out for things that she might like to pick up.
2. *Before* she snatches or sniffs an object, break her focus with a shartp "Eh, eh!" (try to avoid the use of "No"), and if needed a tug on the leash.
3. As she passes the item, say *"Leave it!"* (Remember, not harshly—this should be in the business-like friendly tone.)

4. Praise and treat her as you walk away from the item.

As you repeat this command over days and weeks of walking, you will find that your Boxer will quickly learn what *"Leave it"* means, and you will be able to use it in other circumstances, too, such as when she spots a cat across the street and is thinking about dragging you along with her for a good chase.

Kisses/Hugs

Boxers *love* their people and are known for their excited and boisterous hellos. The wild jumping and licking that accompanies the typical Boxer greeting is O.K. in some instances, but if you are easily toppled, tend to wear clothes that you preferred weren't "signed" with muddy paw prints, or if you have guests, you'll want to control this exuberant greeting. The *kisses/hugs* command allows your Boxer to greet you when you want her to and in a more controlled manner.

Teaching the Kisses/Hugs

1. When your dog is leaping in the air, wild with excitement, say her name and put her in a *sit*. (She must be good at the *sit* for you to teach the second part of this exercise.)
2. Now that she is in a *sit*, pat your chest with your hands and say *"Kisses"* or *"Hugs,"* allowing her to slurp and hug you.

3. When you've had enough, and before your Boxer becomes too excited again, put her back in a *sit*.
4. Release and reward with *calm* praise and treats.

Up/Hup

The last command of this chapter that is quite helpful in everyday living is the *up* or *hup* command. The command is useful when asking your Boxer to jump into your car, or onto a steady, solid grooming table.

Teaching the Up/Hup

1. Pat the surface you'd like your dog to jump to, such as the back of an SUV, a couch, etc. The best surfaces to begin teaching this command to your Boxer are usually those that are low and easy for her to hop up on, and a surface she would *really* like to be on, such as a couch with a dog blanket on it, or perhaps a corner of the bed.
2. As she jumps onto the surface, say "*Up!*" or "*Hup!*"
3. Praise and treat her.

It's as simple as that! With repetition, your dog will follow this command on virtually any surface and anywhere.

10 *Five Boxer Tricks*

In addition to the basic commands and a few helpful everyday words to teach your Boxer, you might also want to teach him a few tricks. The easiest way to teach tricks is to start with those that incorporate behaviors that your Boxer does naturally, particularly those that he does when he's happy or excited. For example, if he enjoys spinning around in circles, you can "teach" him to spin on command by giving the command "*Spin*" or "*Dizzy dog*" whenever you catch him spinning naturally. A reward and praise will cement the link between the verbal command and behavior over a period of time.

The following tricks do, for the most part, require your Boxer to be steady in a few of the basic commands, such as *"Sit"* and *"Down."* Make sure you have the preliminary commands mastered before adding the building blocks necessary to accomplish the trick.

Speak *and* Hush

Some dog owners worry that teaching their dogs to "speak" or bark on command will create a dog that won't stop barking. In actuality, the *speak* and *hush* commands can often be used to curb a talkative Boxer's vocalness because now you have more control, or an "on/off" switch. Additionally, because many Boxers bark for attention (when the Boxer is barking at *you*, that is) or out of boredom, teaching the *speak* and *hush* commands provides interaction with you, which may be exactly what your Boxer needs, and will help to mold a quieter dog.

Speak

The *speak* command can be quite an entertaining trick. If you teach a very subtle hand signal for the command (and your Boxer is *really* tuned in to hand signals), you can have him "answer" questions with a bark, or amazingly "count" with barks.

The speak command can serve a more serious role, too. If part of the reason that you purchased a Boxer was to deter strangers, teaching him to speak can create the appearance of a protective dog—without having any fear of accidental aggression. How does this work? When you teach your Boxer to speak, use a verbal command, such as *"Watch him!"* The threatening stranger will have no idea that your Boxer is barking away with a happy bark rather than a defensive bark; only *you* will be able to tell the difference.

Teaching the Speak

1. Start with a quiet Boxer that isn't barking.
2. Find a way to make him "play bark." For example, if he likes food, one of the easiest ways to get him to bark can be to playfully tease him with a favorite toy or a bit of food. (Your body language is important, too, in that you must relate to him that you're happy and ready to play but won't play until he barks.) For other Boxers, it may be as simple as just a certain "look" that gets him all wound up. Whatever works for you and your dog, as long as it's fun and positive (*never* anything that is frightening or painful!), try to get him to bark.
3. Time the command *with* the bark. When you see a bark coming and you're 99 percent sure he's going to give you a bark—and if you're around your Boxer you pretty well know what that looks like—give the command "*Bark,*" "*Speak,*" or "*Watch him!*" as he begins his bark.
4. Praise and treat your Boxer when he barks, even if he gives just a little "woof" and not a full bark. This will come!
5. Add a hand signal. As your Boxer learns to bark on command, add a hand signal, which can be as simple and subtle as touching your chin or raising your index finger up and down. When he learns the hand signal, fade away the voice command.
6. Follow up the bark command with a *hush* command (see the following).
7. Do not reward "free" barking. Boxers are really wily canines, and if a Boxer links together the fact that he can get a treat every time you tell him to bark, he may just try barking on his own to see if *that* pleases you, too—and that might mean a treat for him. Whatever you do, don't treat him for barking unless you've given him the command to bark.

If your Boxer is barking on his own for a treat, ignore him. Give him the *hush* command (if you've taught him this) or wait until he is quiet, then reward him.

Hush

Equally as important when teaching your pet the *speak* command is training him to stop barking. He needs to learn that he can get treats and praise for being quiet when you ask him, too. Teaching the hush command requires a bit of timing and some patience, but it can be taught through positive reinforcement and repetition.

Teaching the Hush

1. Catch your Boxer when he's quiet. If you've given him the *speak* command and he has barked, you have also rewarded him for speaking. While he is holding his toy in his mouth or munching on his treat, say "*Hush*" and reward him again.
2. If you'd like, add a hand signal, such as the classic index finger to the lips, to the verbal command "*Hush.*" Gradually fade the verbal command away while continuing to reinforce the hand signal with treats.

3. Do not reward barking when the *hush* command has been given. If necessary, put him in a *down-stay* and then give the command "*Hush.*" It is very difficult for a dog to bark while in a *down*, and this may be the edge you need to get your Boxer to *hush*.
4. You can also use a treat to help silence your Boxer. Hold a treat in the palm of a closed hand. It is *very* hard for him to bark while sniffing. At the moment he stops barking, reward him with the treat, and *then* give the command "*Hush.*"

Play Dead (Roll Over) *or* Bang!

If you've got a Boxer that loves to clown around—and a dog that enjoys his treats— this can be a fairly easy trick to teach. As with other tricks, it takes some patience and timing, and of course, lots of praise!

Teaching the "Bang"

1. Put your Boxer in a *down*.
2. With a treat in one hand, hold the treat under your Boxer's nose, then move it slowly back toward one shoulder, around toward the shoulder blades, to encourage him to roll over on his back. As he contorts a bit to follow the treat, or if he is a natural clown, he should be legs up and on his back.

Note: If you're working with a small puppy, you can actually help roll the pup over a little—if he's willing.

3. Say the command, "*Play dead*" or "*Bang!*" when your dog is on his back.
4. The hand signal should be, of course, a finger pointing like a gun!
5. As your dog masters this trick, he may even be able to drop from a standing position to the "dead dog" position for an even more dramatic show.

Note: If your Boxer is a bit fearful or perhaps a bit dominant, this trick may be difficult to teach initially. The reason for this is that dogs that do not trust their masters completely tend to be hesitant to expose their underbellies. (Lying on the back is a submissive gesture that is not seen often in dominant dogs, or in dogs too fearful to lie in such a vulnerable position.)

Shake

A raised paw is a very friendly gesture for a dog, and for the Boxer, friendliness comes quite naturally. Take advantage of this gesture and teach your Boxer the *shake* command.

Teaching the Shake

1. Put your Boxer in a *sit-stay*.
2. Often, all you have to do is extend your hand to your Boxer, palm up, and the puppy or dog will mimic the behavior and lift his paw. Reward and praise any raised paw movement, but do not give the verbal command yet.

3. If your Boxer does not willingly give you a paw, gently touch his leg from behind on his pastern. If a light touch doesn't get him to lift his paw, gently lift the paw for him. Reward and praise.
4. Continue shaping the lifted paw, rewarding and praising him when he offers a higher paw lift each time. When the paw is finally in the correct position for *shake*, shake his paw and say "*Shake.*"

Dance

This trick takes advantage of the Boxer's willingness to jump up but adds control by requiring the Boxer not to touch you with his front paws. The skill is in learning to make a complete turn while on his hind legs—and many Boxers will be able to give you two or three turns!

1. With your Boxer on leash, hold a treat over his head. The treat should be just high enough to encourage the Boxer to stand on his hind legs but not so high that he has to leap to get it— because he will leap!

2. If your Boxer is confused, he may try to *sit*. Be careful not to "correct" him for sitting; rather, tug upward on the leash to encourage him to jump up and not *sit*.
3. When he stands, reward him with praise and give him the treat.
4. Repeat and reward.
5. As he understands that a slight tug means for him to stand on his hind legs, ask him to stand and *follow* the treat. Try to get him to turn 90 degrees while standing on his hind legs.
6. Continue working with him and rewarding him for making progress until you can get him to make a full revolution. When he is making this full spin, associate the command *"Dance!"* with the end of the spin.
7. Continue to associate the verbal command with the full spin and reward for each completion.
8. Continue to associate the hand movement (your hand will already be moving in a circle to get the dog to spin, so this is an easy hand signal to associate with the trick) so that your Boxer will dance to either a voice command or a hand signal.

Biscuit Balance

The Biscuit Balance is sure to delight and amaze your friends and family, as most dogs like to snatch their treats—not balance them on their noses. The *Biscuit Balance*, of course, teaches more than a really cool trick; it also teaches your dog to have patience. This patience will transfer into other areas of your dog's training.

> ### High-Five Variation
> Kneel in front of your Boxer so you are at the same level as he is. Extend your hand, palm up, keeping it low to the floor, and encourage him to touch it with his paw. (This is similar to Targeting, page 20–21.) When he touches his paw to your hand, reward and praise him.
>
> As he understands that you want him to tap his paw to your hand, move your palm to the right, left, back, and forward, asking for a paw tap each time. Reward and praise every paw tap.
>
> Now, try raising your hand up in a very low, high-five position. He should try to tap his paw on your open palm. Reward and praise.

1. Put your Boxer in a calm *sit*.
2. Gently hold your Boxer's muzzle.
3. Reward him with praise and a treat. Repeat until you can gently hold his muzzle for a couple of seconds.
4. Now, while holding your Boxer's muzzle, place a biscuit on his nose, right at the broadest point in front of his eyes.
5. Tell him "Wait, wait," and then release his muzzle while saying "Okay!" Allow him to eat his biscuit and praise him!
6. Continue to practice this skill until he learns that "Wait" means he cannot flip his biscuit to eat it until you release him. Slowly release the grasp on his muzzle, too, so that he will wait even when not being held.

11 *Looking for Trouble*

When you combine the Boxer's extreme intelligence, high activity level, and uncanny sense of humor, you have a dog that must be kept active both physically and mentally. If she isn't, she will find ways to keep herself amused. Unfortunately, the types of things a Boxer tends to think up to keep herself busy rarely amuses her owner. In other words, a bored Boxer, as you might already know, can be a destructive thing.

Idle Boxers have been known to chew, bark, dig, climb, and jump. Because these dogs are so athletic and strong, they tend to perform these destructive activities with great skill, too. That means that the entire couch instead of just a pillow, is shredded, the barking is louder, the holes are bigger and deeper, and fences are scaled with ease.

What's a poor Boxer owner to do?

The best way to solve any or all of these problems is to look beyond the symptoms (barking, digging, climbing, jumping) and treat the cause of the behavior. In other words, if you can figure out the reason *why* your Boxer is doing what she's doing, you most likely can cure or at least minimize the problem behavior.

Exercise and Mental Stimulation—The Best Boxer Cures

Boxers are high-energy dogs, and they are exceptionally intelligent. This breed needs to be challenged both physically and mentally to be truly happy.

Exercise. Daily rigorous walks and/or jogs are a necessity with this breed. High-speed games of fetch should be in addition to, not a substitute for, walks and jogs. When a Boxer is tired, she is much more likely to rest quietly than to go looking for inappropriate activities.

Mental Exercise. Training! This mentally challenges your boxer, and she *loves* this. Train every day. Keep the sessions short and frequent with a puppy, and just long enough when working with an adult that you leave your Boxer wanting *more*.

> ### TRACY'S TIPS
> The Boxer has a heavy exercise need. This can't be stressed enough. This is a dog that just doesn't need a walk, she needs vigorous exercise.

Train tricks, too. Keep it fun. Keep it fresh. Keep changing it up. There's no reason why you can't do "formal" obedience, agility, or rally exercises along with a few tricks, too. And no one says you can't intersperse just plain *play* in your training, too.

In addition to training, it's important to provide mental stimulation even during your Boxer's down time. When she's relaxing in her dog crate, provide her with an interactive toy, such as one that she has to work to get a treat to pop out, or a stuffed Kong with healthy cheese or peanut butter that she has to lick and chew to work out.

Attention. In the process of providing mental and physical stimulation, you have provided something else your Boxer craves—interaction with you. As a working breed, your Boxer wants to be active with you. The more your Boxer is able to "work" with and for you, the less likely she is to become bored and destructive.

Options for Working Owners

If meeting your dog's exercise needs is tough because of your work schedule, consider these options.

1. **Give Your Dog a Break.** If you work close to your home, take your lunch hour with your Boxer. Go home, throw a ball, or take her for a walk. This will help to burn off a little of that Boxer energy and it's a great midday stress buster for you.

2. **Hire a Pet Walker.** Professional pet walkers are great; they take your dog to a local park, play ball with her, or just go for long walks. For an hour every day, she can frolic to her heart's content. This option doesn't come without a price, however. Pet walkers can charge up to $15 a visit for their services in larger cities. If you have a neighbor (perhaps someone is retired in your neighborhood?) or nearby relative who would enjoy walking your dog every day, you might be able to negotiate a better price.

3. **Consider a Doggie Day Care Facility.** This is a full-day service and requires a very sociable dog with no dog-dog aggression and good "pack" behaviors. Screen your day care facility carefully; not all are created equally. Charges are high for this service; you can expect to pay up to $20 a day or more in some areas.

4. **Load Up on Toys.** There are lots of durable, tough toys on the market that will keep your Boxer occupied for sometimes several hours at a time and that can be left safely in her crate when she's unsupervised. Particularly popular are large, hard rubber toys with slots that can be stuffed with biscuits or treats; she will work a long time to get those treats out!

5. **Buy a Crate.** If your Boxer has a serious tendency toward chewing, barking, digging, or climbing fences, crate her when you cannot supervise her. Most dogs enjoy their crates if they are well exercised, have a comfortable surface to lie on, and are given a good chew (see Crate Training, page 76).

6. **Leash Her.** If your Boxer puppy looks for trouble *while* you are home, tie her leash to your belt so that you can have your hands and mind free to attend to other things, but also have a physical tie to her. In other words, she can't run and rip up a couch cushion if she's by your side.

Indoor and Outdoor Behavior Problems

Sometimes you can be doing the best job anyone could hope to do as an owner, and your Boxer will still find ways to wreak havoc in your home and yard.

TRACY'S TIPS

Just as the "death" of an obedience Boxer is boredom, boredom also links over to destructive behaviors. Destructive Boxers can have a short lifespan in a home that doesn't understand the root of this destructiveness. A great pet can wind up being rehomed because she wasn't challenged enough mentally.

The following are some tips and training tools for several of the most commonly cited Boxer problems.

Barking

Boxers don't tend to be barkers, but they can be vocal dogs. They are known for barking a resounding alert when someone has come to the front door. They also can bark for attention, or bark to guard their territory, or bark just for the sheer joy of barking.

- A good way to teach your Boxer when to stop barking in the home is by teaching the dog the *speak* and *hush* commands (see *Speak* and *Hush*, page 117). If your dog knows she will be rewarded

for sounding the alarm, as well as for quickly calming down and becoming silent, she will be much easier to quiet down when you want her to.

- If a dog is barking for attention, you need to take a look at your situation. Be honest. Are you giving this dog enough attention? Or, are you short-changing her a little? If you are, try to increase your activity time with her. Play ball in the backyard, allow her to follow you around the house and "help" with chores, take her on car rides, let the kids take her for walks (if they are ten or older and if she is good at walking on a leash).
- Remember, don't reinforce barking behavior. If she barks for attention, ignore her until she's quiet again, and then lavish the attention.
- Teach a *down*. It's difficult for a Boxer to bark when she's in a full *down* and not up off her elbows (see *Down*, page 103). Once you've got her quiet again, remove her from the source of her barking.

Boxers were bred to be excellent watch dogs, so they shouldn't be punished for alerting you to something, such as a stranger approaching the front door, a dog outside the backyard fence, or the neighbor up on a ladder next door.

You do, however, want to be able to turn your Boxer's alert "off" when you want. Here are some strategies to working with territorial barkers.

- Teach a solid recall. When you call your dog and she turns and leaves the stimulus, her barking is not rewarded because *she* is leaving.

- Remove her from the stimulus. Don't allow your Boxer access to the front door when you aren't home or able to "hush" her, put her in a *down*, or recall her. Crate her or gate off the entryway.
- Take her out. Anecdotally, it appears the more our Boxer is out and away from her home, the less territorial she becomes of her yard and home.
- Exercise her—lots. There's that pesky exercise notation again. Exercise won't stop your Boxer from alerting you, but it may take the edge off her territorial barking and make her more willing to listen to your commands.
- Neuter the Boxer. If your intact male Boxer is particularly territorial (and he is well trained, exercised, and goes out a lot), consider neutering him. This could deflate some of his territoriality towards other dogs.

Exception. There's an exception to the "ignoring" method toward barking. If you attempt to keep her as an outside dog, she *will* bark and she will likely not stop barking until you let her inside the home. And, in this instance, she is right! The Boxer's place is by her owner's side and as a house pet, not a yard ornament. The reason for the barking in this instance is that she is not getting the care and attention she deserves and is letting her owner know.

Chewing

Boxers are big on chewing. They chew as puppies during their teething phase. They chew as young adolescents just because it feels good and is fun. They chew as adults for the same reasons as adolescents, only now that they're fully grown, their bite, which is substantial, is capable of doing a lot of damage.

Chewing is a natural dog thing; it really isn't a bad habit at all—it keeps the dog's teeth clean and white—unless, of course, the Boxer is chewing on something inappropriate, such as your baseboards, leather shoes, or furniture. The good news is that chewing does not have to be a problem. There are several things you can do to help appease your Boxer's healthy appetite for chewing while rescuing your furniture and rugs.

- Keep your Boxer satisfied with a variety of hard rubber chew toys, stuffable chew toys, knotted rope tugs, and chew snacks (Note: Look for chews approved by the Veterinary Oral Health Council [VOHC]).
- Rotate the toys and chews. If you can afford it, keep a bucket of about 12 different chews and toys but only let your dog play with eight at a time. Pick the

chews and toys up at night and give your dog a different mix the next day.

■ Never leave your Boxer unattended. If you *know* you have an active chewer, be sure to crate her or confine her to a trouble-free area of the house when you can't keep your eye on her. Remember, this is a very curious and active dog. Just because something doesn't look like a chew toy to *you* (e.g., the arm of your favorite recliner or a seat belt in your car), doesn't mean it doesn't look like fun to your Boxer.

■ If your Boxer is a really hard chewer, look for toys and chew bones designed for destructive chewers. Avoid shin bones or other hard bones that could chip or break teeth (that's a canine dental bill you'll want to avoid!)

■ Teach your Boxer the *out* command (see page 112). It is not a matter of *if* your Boxer will find something inappro-

> **TRACY'S TIPS**
>
> *The purpose of giving your Boxer a chew or toy is to keep him occupied for a length of time—not just a few minutes. Consider freezing his meals in stuffable hard rubber toys designed for heavy chewers, and make him work to chew the food out. Other options could include canine puzzles, interactive toys, and toys that dispense treats and are made for heavy chewers.*

priate to chew but *when*. Be ready to easily extract the item by being able to ask for it.

■ Keep any room your Boxer has access to picked up and free of loose items, such as shoes, socks, toys, books, newspapers, or magazines on the floor. Make sure the closet door is closed.

■ If your Boxer is honing in on one particular area of the house (perhaps chewing a certain corner of your kitchen cabinets), you can try applying a "no chew" type ointment or spray on the area. The ointment is harmless to dogs, but it has a bitter enough taste that dogs are generally repelled by it. If you are unfortunate enough to own a Boxer with "bad" taste or one with no taste at all, she may like or ignore the ointment, in which case you're back to square one—supervise or crate or contain her in a safe place.

■ Don't "chew" on your Boxer for chewing something up. This won't keep her from chewing again! Remember,

chewing is a natural urge. Your job is to channel this urge by giving her chewing-appropriate items and to supervise!

Digging

Boxers will generally dig for one of several reasons: to bury things, to dig things up (newly planted annuals nearly always need uprooting), to escape underneath a fence, to find a cool spot in the yard on a hot day, or just for the fun of it. Bored dogs may dig more, but it's probably safer to say that unsupervised Boxers dig the most.

If you have a digging dog, there are several things you can try to put a damper on the digging.

■ Bring your dog inside. If she's not outside, she can't dig.
■ Supervise your dog. When your Boxer is outside, watch her. If she starts to dig, tell her *"No!"* or *"Ah-Ah!"* Then distract her with a constructive game of catch or a controlled game of tug.
■ Barricade your yard. If you don't want your Boxer relandscaping for you, build a side yard just for your dog, or protect your plants with an additional fence. Sometimes invisible fences—electric fences buried under the ground that work with a collar—within a large backyard can be very effective in keeping your Boxer in just the areas you want her.
■ Make a digging pit. Now this is only for the brave owner, but it does work for dogs that dig solely to bury and unearth treasures. Construct a 4 × 4 foot (122 × 122 cm) area of soft dirt or sand and bury bones for her. Praise her

when she digs and buries things in this area, and prevent her from doing this elsewhere in the yard. (This requires supervision.)
■ Take the fun out of digging. If your dog is digging to escape under a fence, make sure the areas at the base of the fence are not fun or easy to dig. Large, heavy, rough rocks could make a good border to prevent diggers from escaping.

Climbing

This habit is a frustrating one. It is safe to say that Boxers often scale enormous and seemingly impossible fences just to get to the other side. Unneutered male Boxers are probably the worst offenders and will go to great lengths to leave any form of enclosure if they sense there's a female in season even remotely close to them. Fence climbing is a dangerous sport for a Boxer, and a loose Boxer is very likely to be hit by a car.

If you have a fence climbing Boxer, take heart; there are some ways to dampen your dog's abilities.

■ Alter your Boxer. If you have a male, neuter him. If you have a female, spay her. With no hormonal drive, your Boxer's wanderlust will be dampened.
■ Heighten your fencing. If your fence is only 4 feet (122 cm) tall, this is a piece of cake for your Boxer. Raise it to 6 feet (183 cm) and see if you can stop the problem.
■ Change your fencing. If you have chain link, your Boxer may be able to get a foothold in the links. Consider chang-

ing your fencing to a board fence so she can't get a toehold to begin scaling.

■ Add a slant. If you already have a board fence that your Boxer is climbing, consider reinstalling it with a slight slant *into* the yard. This makes it impossible for her to climb.

■ Charge it. Add an invisible fence and collar system to your already existing fence, but remember, if you have a lot of storms that knock out your power, when the power's down, so is your fence. Also, some Boxers may be so determined to scale the fence, they might suffer the charge just to get out.

■ Put a lip or lid on it. You can try adding a 2-foot (61-cm) "lip" of chain link (if you have a metal fence) or wood to the top of your fence to keep your Boxer contained. Or, if you have a chain link fence, you could consider creating a shaded run area or side yard with a chain link cover to keep your errant Boxer contained when you can't supervise her outdoor play time.

■ Lock her up. Boxers are notoriously good escape artists and this includes an uncanny ability to open gates, twist doorknobs, or do whatever it takes to free themselves. Make sure your gates' latches are locked securely.

Note: A tie-out should never be used with a Boxer for several reasons. First, the Boxer is so strong that if she hits the end of the cable at full strength, she can pull up the stake, and/or severely injure herself. Additionally, an unsupervised dog on a tie-out is inviting trouble. If your Boxer doesn't successfully strangle her

cable is attached to her collar), or injure a leg by wrapping the cable around herself, she might very well develop aggressive tendencies while on the line, based on the fear that she can't escape. When the flight/fight response kicks in, her only option on a line is to fight.

People Problems

For the Boxer, any unwanted behavior problems that affect people generally stem from her unbridled enthusiasm or her profound love and affection for people. (Oh yes, and *lack* of exercise . . .). These behaviors are typical for a dog, but they must be reined in to make her a pet that can be enjoyed by all people.

Jumping Up

The airborne, full-tongue slurp is classic Boxer. This is what Boxer owners live for. There can't possibly be a breed with a warmer, more enthusiastic, know-no-limits kind of welcome. However, if you are dressed and ready for work, carrying in a load of groceries, or introducing a frailer family member to your Boxer, then jumping up becomes a problem.

So, recognizing that the Boxer bounce is a sign of affection, you will want to teach her restraint without dampening her spirits. Here are some tips on how to accomplish this.

■ Teach your Boxer the *kisses/hugs* command (see page 114). This will allow you to control her when you need to,

and allow her to express her affections at a more appropriate time.

■ Reinforce the *sit* command (see page 99). If you don't want to allow your Boxer to jump *ever*, make sure you can give her an activity for which she can be rewarded and praised. If she is steady on her *sits*, tell her to sit whenever she is getting the wild urge to jump or whenever she is greeting people. When she sits, reward her calmly, or have the person she is greeting reward her with a treat. Your Boxer will quickly learn that she gets the attention she wants if she sits. You will find that your Boxer, when coming up on a group of people, may actually sit just so she can get the anticipated attention.

■ Leash her. If your Boxer tends to jump up on your children, one way to have quick control over her is to allow her to drag a light leash in the house. Of course, this must be done *only* when you are home and supervising her; otherwise, she will injure or strangle herself. When she runs up to your child, step on the leash to stop her from jumping, then put her in a *sit* or a *down*. Reward her when she obeys. She will soon learn that she only gets pats and rewards when she sits or lies down for your children.

Nipping and Mouthing

If there is one puppy complaint that seems to exist for all breeds, it is that the puppy is nipping or chewing on her owners. Boxers are no exception to this complaint. Boxers are, as already noted, a breed that likes to chew a lot, and puppies need to learn that human hands, feet, legs, clothing, and shoes are *not* on the list of nippable items. Those little white teeth are like needles and they hurt! Of course, if a child squeals (in pain), the exuberant Boxer often misinterprets this as an invitation for wild play. And, you don't want this behavior to continue as an adult dog.

There are several gentle ways to teach your puppy not to chew on you. The following provide some tips to help you get started working with your puppy to curb her nipping tendencies and to continue to teach her what is called "bite inhibition."

- Provide an alternate behavior. If your puppy or adult is bouncing up and nipping you, tell her *"Ow!"* followed by a *sit* command. Reward a good *sit* with calm praise and then release him, *calmly*.
- Bite this! If you know your Boxer will greet you with nips, head her off at the pass and provide an alternative chew

that is constructive. Have a bone or chew toy ready and, giving her the *take it* command (see *Take It*, page 112), hand the toy to her before she starts nipping you. Often this is enough to head off the nips. After providing a toy several times, you may find that she will actually fetch a toy and bring it to you when she sees you.

- Burn it off. A lot of horsing around can be minimized by allowing your Boxer lots of opportunity to burn off her extra energy. A tired Boxer is often a content Boxer!
- Use time-outs judiciously. If the nipping and mouthing are part of your Boxer's wild greetings, you may want to use her crate (without toys) for a few minutes as a calming area. Do not drag her to the crate as a punishment. Simply coax her gently and calmly to her area and allow her to settle down in the crate.

Resource Guarding

Resource guarding is the unwillingness (by a dog) to give up a coveted item or resource, such as something stolen from the garbage, a favorite chew toy, or even an empty plastic jug. What the Boxer regards as a precious resource that she is willing to protect sometimes defies logic. (A roll of toilet paper? Really?) But protect she will, and depending on how serious she is about not giving the item up, the Boxer may guard the item with snarls, growls, snaps, and even a bite.

Resource guarding can turn ugly very quickly. Resource guarding, however, is a dog behavior. If you have multiple dogs, this is what a dog may do to keep the other dogs from stealing her bone. It's not acceptable behavior, however, when the Boxer decides to guard an item from her human family—particularly if there are children in the home who aren't aware of what the dog is doing and try to pull their plastic action figure out of the mouth of a resource-guarding adult dog.

Resource guarding is something that can be prevented (in part) and managed with dogs that have certain coveted items. If you have small family members, *everyone* must understand how to work with the dog to avoid an accidental injury. And let's point out here that most Boxers do not have this issue, but it's always wise to understand what it is, how to prevent it, and how to manage it should the behavior occur.

Body Language

First, it's important to recognize the body language that a dog that is resource guarding typically exhibits. When the dog has the item, she will often run off with it, and you may not realize she has the item. When you go to find the Boxer, she may have the item—let's say she has a paper fetish and grabbed the empty toilet paper roll, tucked under her chest (as if hiding it) or resting her head and chin on top of it. The look of the Boxer may be a bit threatening and aggressive; however, often times the dog appears more stressed and anxious. That is because this behavior is not necessarily that of a dominant dog. In fact, it is often seen in more timid dogs

that frequently have things taken away from them by other dogs or are observed waiting for other dogs to finish eating before they eat.

Also, many dogs that resource guard are perfectly fine with your taking away a whole host of items from them with no issues. *It's just this one thing…* And as noted previously, the highly coveted item might not be that juicy steak bone stolen from the garbage can but rather a specific type of rubber ball, an empty plastic water bottle, or a balled up piece of paper from the trash can. It doesn't necessarily make sense to us, and it's often a particular item that the dog picks to guard.

Regardless of the motivation for the resource guarding, if you try to snatch the item away, you will be met by a snarl, a clamping down of the chin on the item, or a serious growl. If the item is not in the dog's mouth, the Boxer can more easily snap or bite, too. If you grab the item or the dog drops her hold on the item, she may also bite your hand. Or, the dog may grab the item, run farther away, and continue to make some pretty ugly sounds and display threatening body language.

What now?

Handling the Situation

First, don't panic or yell or holler; this may cause the situation to escalate. Assume a confident and calm but firm demeanor. If you have children, *do* keep them away for the moment. Then, use the following strategies:

1. **Give the *out* command.** If your Boxer is trained to release an item on command, give her the *out* command. Though this command won't prevent her from trying to guard an item, she *will* drop it for you when asked. Teach her the *out* command (see page 112) early on in her training. Really work on it and make sure she is responsive to this command.

2. **Offer a swap.** If the *out* command fails, be prepared. Have a very good treat to offer the Boxer in exchange for the item she is holding. When she drops the item, say *"Out!"* to reinforce the command. *Praise* her for releasing the item. (This last part is hard but very necessary! Don't punish her for releasing the item.)

3. **Walk him.** *If* the Boxer is showing no aggression (no growling, snarling,

hackles, hardened eyes, or stress) but simply won't swap the item for the yummy treat, you can loop a leash over her head or clip one on to her collar and start walking her. Keep your treats with you and start making her perform *sits* and *walk nicely*. Eventually, she will drop the item.

4. **Take the item away *permanently*.** If you know what your Boxer is likely to guard, make sure to keep these items away from her. If she tends to guard chew bones (and you *want* her to chew and eat a specific dental bone), only offer her this item when she's in her crate and she stays in her crate until she's eaten the edible bone. She is alone and undisturbed in her crate. She is not being rewarded for bad behaviors because she is not offering these behaviors in her crate.

5. **Teach your children the rules from the get-go.** When a child is bitten, it really doesn't matter what events led up to the bite; it is devastating for the family and often means a lack of trust with the Boxer and a loss of a good home. Help your Boxer to succeed by requiring your children to respect the dog. They are *not* to pull things out of the dog's mouth—even if it's the child's toy. The child comes to *you* to retrieve the item. Children are not allowed to go in the dog's crate; that's the dog's rest area. And, children should not put their faces in the dog's face, nor should they disturb the dog or reach into the dog's bowl while she's eating.

6. **Food bowl tips.** To prevent a pup from guarding her food bowl, get her used to people reaching into her bowl

(which, of course, you've told your kids *not* to do but they will probably do it anyway). While the puppy is eating, drop a little piece of yummy cooked chicken breast into her bowl. ("Oh wow! A hand near my bowl means a treat is coming!") Practice this every time you feed your Boxer, and she will quickly associate the incoming hand—whether it has a treat or not—as something good.

If a dog already has food bowl issues, stop feeding her from her bowl and start hand feeding her—and make her perform tasks. She needs to earn her dinner, and she learns that the food comes from you—that you're the source of her food, you're not the one taking her food away. After she readily eats from your hands and performs tasks, you can begin feeding a portion of her food to her *while she's in her crate.*

Is This More than Resource Guarding?

A Boxer that is just "funny" about one particular item is very predictable, and the entire issue of resource guarding can be avoided by never allowing the dog to have that one certain item. She's a perfect dog otherwise, and she's completely wonderful with kids, other dogs, the family, and neighbors.

But, what if your Boxer is growling and snarling with every item she has? Or, what if she's protective of her food but there's another element going on here that you can't quite figure out? If you've ever got a feeling that something else is going on, or if your Boxer scares you on any level, you should seek the opinion of a professional.

Consult with your veterinarian and describe all the behaviors that are concerning you. It could be that your Boxer may benefit from a stronger leadership role from you and some good ol' obedience training—and lots of exercise to diffuse pent-up energy. And then again, you could have the rare Boxer that has some aggression issues and needs more examination from a behaviorist or experienced trainer to develop a plan of action.

Whatever you do, don't turn a blind eye to the problem. It won't go away, and whatever is going on will simply escalate over time. It's easier to get help when a problem is first noticed than to let it reach a point where only a highly skilled trainer can manage the problem.

12 *Activities*

Noncompetitive Activities

The Boxer is a working breed, which means she lives to work for you. If you'd like to take a step beyond training your dog for good manners and a few tricks, there are many activities in which you can become involved with your Boxer.

The first half of this chapter covers the noncompetitive activities in which Boxers excel, along with some ideas on getting started in these activities and some beginning training tips. For those who enjoy the thrill of competing, the second half of the chapter covers several events in which you may be interested in training your dog to compete both with Boxers and other breeds or mixes of breeds.

For additional information and listings of related organizations on any or all of the activities listed in this chapter, consult the Useful Addresses and Literature section at the end of this book.

AKC S.T.A.R. Puppy Program

The S.T.A.R. (Socialization, Training, Activity, Responsibility) program from the AKC was developed to encourage new puppy owners to get involved with their puppies and learn the basics of training and to learn about socialization with people and dogs, healthcare, and what it takes to be a responsible dog owner. The S.T.A.R. program is considered to be a first step toward training, with the Canine Good Citizen (CGC) (see page 139) designed to be a continuation of the S.T.A.R. program.

To participate in the S.T.A.R. program, puppies and owners must be enrolled in a six-week training program with an approved S.T.A.R. instructor. To find a training class, go to *www.akc.org/starpuppy/*.

Getting Started

The program includes four sections: an owner pledge, which must be read and signed by the owner; an evaluation of the owner's behaviors; an evaluation of the puppy's behaviors; and a "Pre-CGC" behaviors test. It may sound like a lot to take in, but don't worry. These programs are designed to be fun and relaxed and will help you to discover how enjoyable and rewarding training your dog is.

Pledge. The pledge shows that the owner understands a puppy's health needs, nutri-

Pre-CGC test behaviors. At the conclusion of the six-week training program, the puppy and handler will be tested on nine tasks:

1. Allow petting by another person
2. Allow the owner to perform basic grooming and to touch ears and feet
3. Walk on a leash in a straight line for 15 feet (4.5 m)
4. Walk on a leash nicely when walking past other people within 5 feet (1.5 m)
5. *Sit* on command (a food lure can be used)
6. *Down* on command (a food lure is okay here, too)
7. *Come* to owner on command from 5 feet (1.5 m) away
8. React appropriately to distractions 15 feet (4.5 m) away
9. Allow another person to hold the leash while the owner steps 10 feet (3 m) away and returns

tion, regular veterinary care, and exercise and grooming requirements. It also covers dog safety, rights of others, and important quality of life needs such as attention, training, play, and a commitment by the owner.

Owner behaviors. This is an evaluation performed by the S.T.A.R. instructor to figure out if the owner has maintained the necessary vaccination records and is keeping a health record, has developed a daily care and exercise plan, and has properly provided identification (i.e., tags) for the puppy.

Puppy behaviors. This portion of the program evaluates the puppy's social behaviors and basic comfort levels with people and basic training tools, such as a collar or harness and leash. It also tests to see if the puppy will allow the owner to take a treat or toy away and hug or hold the puppy.

What It Takes for S.T.A.R.

- ■ Every Boxer pup enrolled in a puppy training class should be able to participate (and earn his medal!) in the S.T.A.R. program
- ■ Records of vaccinations
- ■ Basic owner education as to health and responsibility
- ■ Good socialization skills
- ■ 12 months or younger; older or more advanced Boxers will need to test for the AKC's CGC certification (though those of unknown youthful age will not be turned away from the S.T.A.R. program)

Canine Good Citizen

This certification was started in 1989 by the American Kennel Club (AKC) with the pet owner in mind. The Canine Good Citizen (CGC) test is sponsored by the AKC and tests the basic good manners of a dog, as well as emphasizing responsible pet ownership. The test is pass/fail and is noncompetitive. Dogs that pass the CGC receive certification from the AKC, as well as having their names recorded in the AKC's CGC archive. Owners may also elect to purchase CGC collar tags from the AKC that verify that dogs have passed the CGC test.

As previously mentioned, the CGC title is required by some AAA/T organizations for certification as a therapy dog. Additionally, 34 states have Canine Good Citizen resolutions to advance responsible dog ownership, and these numbers are expected to increase. Since its inception, the CGC program has served as a model for programs in other countries, too, including those in England, Australia, Japan, Hungary, Denmark, Sweden, Canada, and France.

Currently, many local police and animal control agencies use the CGC model to help solve dog problems in communities, and a growing number of 4-H groups have adopted the CGC model as a beginning dog training program for children.

Many training schools, 4-H centers, shelters, and even veterinary hospitals offer both training and testing for the CGC. The only requirement for participation in the training and testing programs is that your dog be up to date on his vaccinations. (He doesn't need to be an AKC-registered Boxer; paperless Boxers are welcome!)

Getting Started: Canine Good Citizen

The following are the ten items that your dog will be tested on for the CGC test. Remember, your Boxer must pass *all* ten tests within the CGC to be certified. If you fail one, you will need to wait and practice for at least six months before you can be retested.

Test 1: Accepting a Friendly Stranger. In this test, you and your Boxer will approach a friendly stranger (usually the

and must show neither fearfulness nor aggression.

Test 3: Appearance and Grooming. In this exercise, the evaluator inspects the dog as a veterinarian or a judge might, including brushing him and examining his ears and both front paws.

Test 4: Out for a Walk (Walk on a Loose Leash). The fourth test checks to see if your Boxer will stay with you through a couple of stops, a left turn, right turn, and an about turn. Your Boxer doesn't need to be in perfect *heel* position; in fact, he can be on your left or right, slightly ahead or a little behind you, but he should clearly be attentive. He is also not required to sit when you stop walking.

Test 5: Walking Through a Crowd. This test ensures that your Boxer will successfully navigate a crowd of people. You will be asked to walk and weave your way through a group of people. You may talk to him and encourage him throughout the exercise.

Test 6: *Sit* and *Down* on Command/ Staying in Place. This tests your Boxer's ability to recognize and perform the *sit* and *down* commands, as well as a *sit-stay* or *down-stay*. On the *stay*, you will walk 20 feet (6 m) away from him (while he is on a 20-foot leash) and walk immediately back to him. He must stay in place, but he can change positions (move from a sitting position to lying down or vice versa).

Test 7: Coming When Called. For this, your Boxer must prove he can stay in a *sit-stay* while you walk a distance of 10 feet (3 m) away from him, turn to face him,

test evaluator) to shake hands and chat a little. Your Boxer must not show signs of aggression or fear, and must stay by your side.

Test 2: Sitting Politely for Petting. The second exercise of the CGC requires the friendly stranger to be able to touch your Boxer while he is sitting at your side. The evaluator will stroke your dog on his head and side. He must be in control and then call him. He must come to you (but you can use verbal encouragement).

Test 8: Reaction to Another Dog. In this exercise, you will be required to approach another handler and dog team, stop, shake hands, chat briefly, and then continue on your way, with your Boxer showing only mild curiosity in the other dog.

Test 9: Reactions to Distractions. In this exercise, the evaluator tests your dog's reactions to such sudden noises or events as a large book or pan being dropped, an umbrella being opened, or a runner jogging by. The evaluator looks to see if your dog responds negatively—fearfully or aggressively—to any of these or other situations.

Test 10: Supervised Separation. The final exam is designed to show your dog's ability to allow someone else to hold his leash briefly (three minutes) while you walk away from him. He doesn't have to maintain a *stay*, but he mustn't go berserk when you leave him with someone else.

What It Takes for CGC

- Any Boxer with basic training skills should be able to polish them up enough to achieve the CGC certification.
- Proof of up-to-date vaccinations are needed.
- Good socialization and habituation skills are needed.
- From four months old to 12 years and beyond, any age Boxer can test for this certification.

Animal-Assisted Activities and Animal-Assisted Therapy (AAA/T)

For years studies have indicated that human interaction with pets improves a person's quality of life, including the pet owner's mental and physical health. That's why visiting pet programs are now recognized by many health care facilities to be an integral part of a patient's care plan.

Animal-assisted activities and therapy (AAA/T) is a facet of health care that

involves visits and interaction with a pet. In some settings, AAA/T is treated with as much importance as any other therapy, such as physical, occupational, and speech therapies. The visits are structured and planned according to the individual patient's needs and are supervised by the health care facility. A less structured form of AAA/T is called "pet visitation," in which the visit from the pet is treated as more of a social event.

AAA/T is utilized in a variety of settings, including rehabilitation hospitals, pediatric acute care facilities, long-term nursing care, schools for the disabled, senior shut-ins, at-risk children's programs, hospices, mental health facilities, abuse shelters, orphanages, and even correctional facilities.

Certification requirements for AAA/T and pet visitation vary according to the certifying organization; however, you most likely will be required to achieve a CGC certificate (see Canine Good Citizen, page 139), complete a training class geared toward AAA/T, pass a special test, and complete a one-on-one interview, with your dog, at an AAA/T testing facility.

The AAA/T test typically involves the dog's acceptance of a variety of situations she might encounter in a working therapy situation, such as a rolling wheelchair, a dropped pan, loud or sudden shouting, and uncontrolled movement. The potential therapy dog will also be tested on his reactions to some uncomfortable situations, such as a toe that is stepped on, a pulled ear, or a tug on her skin. Some certifying organizations may require that you and your Boxer take an aptitude test to evaluate for what type of setting you are best suited.

Many organizations, such as obedience clubs, kennel clubs, shelters, humane societies, and local AAA/T organizations, offer testing and certification for therapy work with a national organization. Recertification is generally required every couple of years, depending on the certifying organization. It is essential for liability reasons that you and your Boxer receive this certification if you wish to pursue this kind of work.

Getting Started: AAA/T

1. **Reinforce Your Boxer's Commands.** Work with your Boxer until he is steady in the basic commands: *sit*, *stay*, *stand*, and *come*. He should also walk nicely on a leash.

2. **Socialize, Socialize, Socialize!** Introduce your Boxer as described in Chapter 5: Socialization. Try to have him meet as many different types of people as possible in a positive way.

3. **Go Everywhere with Him.** The more places you can take him, the more confident your Boxer will be in strange or unusual surroundings. That means take him on walks, up and down flights of steps, into buildings that accept dogs, such as your veterinarian's office. As he gains confidence, take him to more crowded areas, such as a sidewalk in

town during the day. Practice walking on slick surfaces that you are likely to find in institutions.

4. **Groom Him and Bathe Him Regularly.** He will need to be immaculate for his therapy visits, which means you must minimize shedding and keep him tick and flea free. His nails must also be kept short and smooth to prevent any chance of scratching a patient.

5. **Enroll in a Class to Train for a Canine Good Citizen Certificate.**

6. **Locate a Club That Sponsors Testing for AAA/T Certification** (see page 161).

A good resource for locating training and testing facilities, as well as teams of AAA/T dogs and handlers, is the Delta Society. For a less involved or more occasional social pet therapy participation, consider being a "Pet Partner," also through the Delta Society. For information on certification and requirements for both AAA/T and Pet Partners, visit the Delta Society's website at *www.deltasociety.org.*

What It Takes for AAA/T

Does your Boxer have what it takes to become a therapy dog? Here's a brief checklist of qualities to look for.

- Gentleness
- A calm approach to most situations
- Not easily startled (curious is O.K.)
- Steady in basic commands
- Tolerant
- Well-socialized with all sorts of people
- Enjoys physical praise

Search and Rescue

Search and Rescue (SAR) teams are primarily volunteer organizations. (In some areas of the country, fire departments have SAR teams.) This means that handlers and their dogs respond to search for lost people or bodies, generally in areas that are difficult to search with just humans, such as forests, woods, and swamps. SAR teams are also called upon to search in disaster situations, such as the aftermaths of hurricanes, tornadoes, and explosions.

In very simplistic terms, the SAR dog may either be trained to "track," in which the dog finds and follows the actual foot path of the individual, or to "air scent," in which the dog is trained to scent for *any* human or a body and follows in the

direction of the scent. SAR dogs may be taught to work closely with their handler, or to run ahead, find the victim, retrace their path, alert the handler to the find, and then return the handler to the victim. (Boxers during World War I in Germany performed this same function as medic dogs. As mentioned previously in this book, one Boxer was so good at finding wounded soldiers, retracing her steps, and leading medics to the soldiers that she was awarded the Iron Cross.)

Training for SAR requires a group effort: handlers, their dogs, and skilled trainers, who are often handlers, too, along with a corps of volunteers willing to trudge into the woods and wait for the handlers and dogs to find them. SAR handlers must also learn orienteering and survival techniques and pass a series of certifying tests with their dogs before they can work as a SAR team.

Getting Started: Search and Rescue

1. **Find a SAR Club.** One of the most important steps you'll need to take when considering training your Boxer for SAR work is to find a local or area club. Meet with members, talk to them about their dogs, how they train, how often they train, and what is expected of members.

2. **Train with a Mission.** To be a certified SAR team, you will be required to train for and pass a series of tests. Your local club will provide weekly—sometimes even twice a week or more—training sessions and will be able to

guide you to the place you must travel to in order to be tested.

3. **Start Young.** If you have a puppy that is fully vaccinated, you can begin scent training with the SAR club. Many trainers feel that the younger the dog is started in this work, the more focused he is on scenting.

4. **Follow, Follow.** If you have a very young puppy, Norbert Zawatzki, director of training for the German Boxer Club, suggests beginning with a "cookie" trail. "Leave a short trail of little bits of dog cookies in a straight line," he recommends, "and begin your puppy with the first cookie." Encourage your puppy to follow the trail. His reward, of course, is the cookies. Increase the distance in the trail, widening the gap between cookies.

5. Eventually, you can add a corner to your cookie trail and go longer distances. As your puppy progresses in tracking the cookies, you will progress to dragging the cookies a short distance to begin a trail.

What It Takes for SAR

Can the Boxer you own right now make a good SAR dog? It is possible. By nature, this breed possesses a high drive to work. Boxers also have a tremendous sense of smell. These two factors coupled with the Boxer's capacity for learning makes many Boxers potential SAR training candidates. The following is what is needed.

- A healthy, strong dog
- An equally healthy and strong owner
- A dog with lots of energy
- A strong drive to play with toys, which are often used as the rewards

- Good working obedience, though perfection is not necessary
- A dog that is well-socialized with people so that he won't growl, bite, or otherwise attack the "victim" once he or she is found
- An owner who has time to train on weekends and during the week
- An owner with a flexible schedule who is able to be on call 24 hours a day and take off on a moment's notice for a local, regional, or even international search or rescue

Swimming

Swimming is a fun activity for both Boxer and owner. Many of us live near a body of water (pond, lake, river, or ocean) or even have a pool in our backyards. Swim-

ming is also a great activity for a Boxer that is arthritic, recovering from surgery, or suffering from certain immobilizing diseases, such as degenerative myelopathy (DM).

The Boxer, however, as a deep-chested breed, is not naturally suited for swimming. So, whether you are interested in taking him with you to the beach or in your pool, there are some precautions you should take.

Getting Started: Swimming

1. **Invest in a Properly-Fitted Canine Life Jacket.** This will help your Boxer to feel more secure in the water. It will also give you something to grab if you need to pull him out.

2. **Keep It Quiet.** If you are taking your Boxer to the beach, make sure you take her when the ocean is very calm. Booming waves and heavy surf cannot only frighten a dog, but they can also be very dangerous.

3. **Start Young.** The sooner your Boxer is introduced to water, the more likely she will be accepting of this activity. When

he's older and arthritic, he'll thank you for this wonderful form of exercise and therapy!

4. **Make a Slow Water Entry.** Whether you're introducing your Boxer to a pool, lake, or ocean, make the first steps small. Put a small children's turtle pool in your backyard with just enough water to get your puppy's feet wet. Keep it lots of fun to play in the turtle pool! Once he's comfortable in just a little water, increase the amount of water in the turtle pool before progressing to the *real* pool. In the pool, encourage him to step onto the first step with you. Praise him. Step farther into the pool and see if you can entice him farther in with a special toy. When he enters the water, hold his collar gently and grasp him under his chest to help him balance and float next to you. (Watch out for toenails!) Praise him when he starts paddling under water.

5. **Have Patience.** It may take up to eight sessions in the pool before your Boxer begins to figure out that this is really fun. You'll see his progress with every swim though.

6. **Teach the Exit.** Many dogs drown because they fall into pools and can't find the way out. Mark the steps with a visible marker, such as a red flag, and make sure to teach your Boxer where the steps are and exit with him each time this way.

7. **Lock the Gate.** Just as with children of any age, swimming should never be an unsupervised activity. Make sure your Boxer has access to the pool only when you can watch and when he has his life jacket on.

What It Takes for Swimming

Any Boxer should be able to swim if he is introduced slowly to the activity with lots of positive reinforcement, and a life jacket.

Competitive Activities

If you enjoy the thrill of working as a team with your Boxer, and don't mind the heat of competition, or perhaps even thrive upon this kind of challenge, you'll be happy to know that there are many activities in which you and your Boxer might be well suited.

The following gives an introduction to seven popular sports, some tips on getting started, and a checklist of attributes to see if your Boxer might be suited for a particular sport. Additional resources, including sanctioning organizations and further reading, are included in the Useful Addresses and Literature section of this book. And keep in mind that this is just a starter list of sports. New dog sports are being offered every year, making it a very exciting time to own a highly trainable, enthusiastic Boxer!

Agility

Agility is considered to be the fastest-growing dog sport in the United States. It is exciting to watch as a spectator, and even more exciting to participate in as a handler. Agility, in basic terms, is a com-

petition that tests the dog and handler team's ability to negotiate a series of obstacles as fast as possible. The obstacles include tunnels, jumps, weave poles, see-saws, and suspended tires.

The handler's job is to direct the dog using only voice and hand signals through the course. The dog's job is to follow his master's directions as quickly as possible while running off lead. Most dogs, even those that are a bit shy, thoroughly enjoy this sport.

In Canada, the leading Agility organizations include the Agility Association of Canada (AAC) and NADAC.

Many handlers begin Agility classes because they are looking for a fun outlet with their dogs, only to be so caught up in their dogs' enthusiasm for the sport that they decide to enter the competitive scene.

There are currently five major sanctioning organizations in the United States for Agility: the American Kennel Club (AKC), Canine Performance Events (CPE), the North American Dog Agility Council (NADAC), the United Kennel Club (UKC), and the United States Dog Agility Association (USDAA). Titles are awarded by each organization, and the requirements for each vary.

> **TRACY'S TIPS**
> *Obedience is a must for participation in Agility. The basics of obedience are the foundation of Agility.*

All five of the leading Agility organizations allow registered purebred dogs to compete, as well as Boxers with unknown parentage (adopted/rescued), and Boxer mixes. Check with each organization for registration and entry requirements.

Additionally, dogs competing in Agility events must be at least 15 months old to enter.

Getting Started: Agility

1. **Get Grounded.** While you're waiting for your Boxer to be old enough to begin learning the various obstacles involved in the Agility events, take time to teach him to respond *well* to your verbal commands or hand signals. A very obedient dog will have a lot of fun with Agility!

2. **Clear Your Dog.** Make sure your Boxer is free of any hip or other musculoskeletal problems and is in good health. Agility is great fun and provides a good source of exercise, but if he has physical problems, some of the obstacles may exacerbate his condition.

3. **Socialize and Habituate Your Dog.** A confident dog will learn the obstacles of Agility more readily than one that is fearful. If your Boxer is timid, however, participating in Agility will be a big boost to his confidence!

4. **Join an Agility Club.** If you have an enormous yard, time to spare, and money to spend, you could attempt to construct all the equipment used in Agility competitions. Then again, you could choose instead to join an Agility club, take training classes to introduce all the Agility obstacles, practice with other fun members, and use the club's facilities whenever you want. (You can still build a few of the smaller obstacles for backyard practices.)

5. **Never Rush.** Take your time with your Boxer and above all, keep it fun!

What It Takes for Agility

- A healthy dog free of orthopedic problems that is at least 18 months old, preferably 24 months, or older
- Solid obedience skills of *down*, *come*, and *stay*, and the ability to work off leash
- Speed and agility (for competition)
- An owner who is in relatively good shape or who wants to get or keep in shape

Conformation

This is the only competitive event in which looks count. When you enter a Boxer in the conformation ring, a judge will closely examine your Boxer's structure, bite, coloration and markings, physical conditioning, and overall appearance of health and movement. The judge will then compare him to the standard for the breed. The breed standard is a detailed description

written and approved by the American Boxer Club that spells out what a perfect Boxer should look like from head to toe. If, in the opinion of the judge, your Boxer matches the breed standard more closely than the other dogs in the ring, the judge will "put up" or award your dog the winner of his class.

This is in theory, of course. Just as all owners think their Boxer is beautiful, every judge has his or her own preferences within the breed and interprets the breed standard slightly differently. In other words, the world of judging and conformation is subjective.

Since the Boxer is an extremely popular dog, competition in the show ring is stiff. In order to rack up the points needed to attain an AKC championship, he will have to win over a lot of other good-looking Boxers. In AKC shows, you will find yourself pitted against both seasoned owners/breeders, as well as professional handlers—who are paid to *win*. In UKC shows, dogs must be owner handled, so the only professionals in the ring will be those who actually own the dog they are handling. Also, in UKC shows, points are handled a bit differently than in AKC shows. For example, a class winner will be selected; however, if the judge deems all the dogs in a class as outstanding examples of the breed, all worthy dogs will receive points toward their UKC championships.

Regardless of whether you're showing in AKC or UKC shows (or both), showing in conformation requires a lot of time, money, and travel. Though it is more difficult for an amateur owner/handler to show and win with a dog (even when the dog is very good) in AKC shows, it is *not* impossible. A solid dog *will* finish; it just may take a little longer.

Getting Started: Conformation

1. **Evaluate Your Boxer Honestly.** Before you take the plunge to begin training your Boxer for the conformation ring, ask your breeder if he or she feels your dog is capable of attaining a championship. If your breeder is, for some reason, not available to help you, you may be able to find another reputable breeder willing to help you evaluate your Boxer.

2. **Learn the Ropes.** Go to shows and watch carefully how the polished amateur owners and breeders handle their dogs. Learn and understand the point system, as well as the different classes in which you can enter. Talk to other Boxer breeders and owners, listen, and learn.

3. **Learn and Practice "Stacking."** If your puppy is going to make his entrance in the show, he'll have to know how to stand still and keep his feet where you place them. There are dogs that literally can't put a foot down wrong, but most dogs can and do put their feet down in awkward positions which can amplify or bring attention to a fault. Use the *stand-stay* command to keep your Boxer in position, and get him used to you moving his feet into place.

4. **Play Judge.** Have friends and neighbors practice checking your Boxer's teeth, eyes, ears, and body. He will need to stay immobile during this process, which means he can't get too excited or begin to jump around. He also cannot pull back or otherwise shy away from the judge. Any act of aggression will get you and your pet tossed from the ring. Be sure to practice the *stand for examination* with people who smell differently. There have been many stories of dogs that were not timid at all, but would shy away from hands smelling heavily of cigarette smoke or cologne.

5. **Go Through the Paces.** When in the show ring, you will need to be able to "gait" your dog, or trot briskly around the ring to show off your dog's front, back, and side movement. Your Boxer will need to be able to move comfortably on a slender slip collar and lead used for showing—and not drag you around uncontrollably. He will also need to learn (and so will you) the basic gaiting patterns used in the show ring; down-and-back, a triangle, the "L" pattern, and possibly others.

6. **Take a Conformation Class.** The best way to learn the movements of the show ring and to polish your performance is by attending a conformation class with your Boxer. These are typically held by dog breed clubs and are offered on a regular basis.

7. **Go to Fun Matches.** These matches are for fun, literally. They are not official shows, but they can be used for training. You may also be able to get a better idea about whether your Boxer and you really do have what it takes to achieve a championship.

What It Takes for the Show Ring

- Conformation that is as close to the breed standard as possible with few if any faults.
- Good movement. It's not just good enough to "look" good, a potential champion must move well, too.
- Solid temperament. The Boxer that loves to perform in the show ring is generally, with all else being equal, the one who literally demands that the judge "Pick me!"
- Professional presentation. You can have the most gorgeous Boxer in the world, but if you bumble the handling and *look* like an amateur in an AKC show, many judges won't consider your dog. UKC shows are more forgiving of handler errors; however, the more professionally you present your Boxer, the better he will look. So, when you're competing in an AKC or a UKC show, make sure that if you are handling your Boxer, you handle him professionally.
- Winners all. Remember that no matter how your dog does in the ring, he is *your* Boxer and that automatically counts for something in your heart. Treat him like the champion he is, whether or not he wears the title!

Flyball

Flyball is a team sport that packs a lot of excitement into just a few minutes of competition. Flyball enjoys pockets of popularity in the United States, so it is not available everywhere yet. If you have the opportunity to train with a local flyball team, or if you're interested in forming your own team (think of the fun an all-Boxer team would have!), both you and your Boxer will enjoy yourselves.

Flyball involves relay teams of four dogs and handlers. The dogs, one at a time, race over a 51-foot (15-m) course with four hurdles. At the end of the straight course of hurdles is a box. The dog must run to the box and hit a lever with his paw, which hurls a tennis ball up in the air. He must then catch the ball and race

back over the course of jumps to the start, where the next dog on the team takes off.

The winner of each heat is determined by the fastest time weighted against any deductions for errors, such as dropping a ball or missing a jump. Two teams participate in each heat in a single-elimination flyball tournament. Hurdles are set 5 inches (13 cm) lower than the shoulder height of the smallest dog on each team, with a minimum hurdle height of 7 inches (18 cm) and a maximum of 14 inches (36 cm).

The sanctioning organization is the North American Flyball Association. Titles are awarded through this organization and are based on a point system. NAFA reports that there are more than 700 member clubs in North America, Europe, Australia, and other countries, and more than 16,000 dogs registered in the sport.

Getting Started: Flyball

1. **Speed Up the Recall.** In flyball, there is a need for speed. Entire teams (of dogs) are running the 51-foot course in *under* 20 seconds, with world records approaching 15 seconds. One area in which many competitors find they need work is in the speed of the *recall*. Many a dog has been delighted to run to the flyball box knowing that he can pop out a ball, and then be less than enthusiastic to bring the ball back. To speed up your Boxer's *recall*, you can work on the *recall* exercises (see *Come*, page 105).

2. **Encourage the Ball Drive.** The more ball crazy your Boxer is, the faster he's going to run to the ball box. One

way to increase his ball drive is to limit his access to balls. Balls should be perceived as highly prized items and associated with excitement and fast retrieves.

3. **Keep Things Healthy.** Make sure that before you begin participating in flyball, as with any sport, your Boxer is in good health and free of any conditions that might be aggravated by running hard and jumping hurdles.

4. **Find a Flyball Club.** This is a team sport, after all, and the club will have all the necessary equipment, not to mention experience. Find a club at *www.flyball.org*, or receive information on how to start your own club.

What It Takes for Flyball

- No dog-dog aggression
- Enthusiasm and high energy
- A craze for balls
- Good health

Obedience

Competing in obedience trials can be done on two very different personal levels: You can work to attain obedience titles on your Boxer, or you can compete to win or place in your class or trial. Which level you decide to compete at is entirely up to you and your Boxer.

The first level is that of attaining titles. At this level, you have fun working with your Boxer, he has fun working with you, and you aren't as concerned with how

In Canada, rally is offered through the Canadian Association of Rally Obedience and APDT.

high your score is as much as achieving passing scores to earn the "legs" necessary to attain the title. At this level, the only pressure that is on you is the pressure you place on yourself.

At the higher level, you are training your Boxer to be as flawless as possible. Your goal is not merely to pass each judged test, but to score so highly that you are in a position to place in or win your class. You might even have your eye on a "High in Trial" trophy, or perhaps you might be working toward an obedience championship. Depending on your skills as a trainer and your Boxer's potential as an obedience whiz, these goals are not out of sight for you.

In fact, virtually every Boxer—with training of course—should be able to achieve his "Companion Dog" (CD) title. The CD is offered through AKC-sanctioned trials and is the entry level into the world of obedience. (The United Kennel Club also offers obedience trials and titles. See Useful Addresses and Literature for more

information.) If you've never entered a dog in an obedience trial before, you'll be able to enter Novice A. If you've trained a dog and tested at an AKC-sanctioned obedience trial, then you will need to enter Novice B. In order to earn a CD, your Boxer will need to receive passing scores at three different trials under three different judges. A passing score requires a minimum of 170 points out of 200 possible points.

The exercises for the CD title include: *heeling on lead and heeling in a figure 8* (40 points); *off-lead stand for examination* (30 points); *heeling off lead* (40 points); *recall exercise* (30 points); *sit-stay* for one minute (30 points); and *down-stay* for three minutes (30 points).

TRACY'S TIPS
Obedience is the foundation for all sports. No matter what sport you're interested in participating in, your Boxer will need to have a good grounding in basic obedience skills.

153

Getting Started: Obedience

1. **Find a Good Training Club.** You can train your Boxer by yourself using a myriad of books written for both the novice handler and the advanced superstar; however, it is difficult to replicate all the different training scenarios without help. Training clubs also are comprised of trainers and dog owners with a variety of experience, which, if they are willing to share their expertise freely with you, can provide you with a wealth of training tips and problem solving abilities.

2. **Perfect Practice Makes Perfect.** As authors Mary R. Burch, Ph.D. and Jon S. Bailey, Ph.D. so concisely sum up in *How Dogs Learn* (New York: Howell Books, 1999), "'Practice makes perfect' isn't exactly true. *Perfect* practice makes perfect." What this means is that the skilled trainer makes fewer training mistakes and therefore rarely has to back-

track or "undo" inadvertent training errors. When training under a skilled trainer for competitive obedience, you will make fewer mistakes as a trainer, and your Boxer will learn more quickly and with fewer roadblocks.

3. **Keep the Enthusiasm and Attention!** An enthusiastic Boxer performing obedience is an awesome sight.

4. **Take It Slowly.** Don't rush your Boxer. Take it at his speed. Be patient. Sometimes it will seem that you're not making any progress, then the light will shine. Persevere!

5. **Practice Early Heeling Exercises for Focus.** Some animal behaviorists estimate that if a puppy doesn't learn to focus on his master by the time he reaches four or five months old, you will be competing for his attention from then on. This means that your puppy really should be walking nicely on a leash (see *Walk Nicely*, page 108) and focusing on you by the time he is five months old.

6. Introducing Dumbbells Early. If you plan on gaining titles beyond the entry level CD, be sure you introduce dumbbell work to your puppy at an early age. Using a plastic dumbbell, practice the *take it* and *out* commands (see *Take It and Out*, page 112) from time to time. Don't allow your Boxer to play with the dumbbell unsupervised or allow him to chew on it. Rather, make taking and releasing the dumbbell a "special" fun game he can play only with you.

What It Takes for Obedience

- A Boxer. Every Boxer should be able to successfully attain his CD title.
- An enthusiastic, energetic Boxer that is capable of focusing.
- Creative handling. Boxers bore easily and need an owner who can think of ways to keep learning a fun and new experience.
- Patience. Boxers are not ready to focus quite as early as some other breeds, so owners must realize that this process can't be rushed—but keep working at it!

Rally-style Obedience

This sport is similar to obedience; however, the owner and dog team perform all the exercises in one continuous motion. Handlers are allowed to talk to their dogs, as well as praise and encourage them verbally. It's exciting, fast paced, and a lot of fun. Rally is offered by the AKC, APDT, C-Wags, and UKC with similar rules. In

other words, if you train for Rally competitions, you should—with a little practice and knowledge of the different rules—be able to participate in all clubs' events.

Current rules require a Rally course to consist of 25 to 28 different exercises, depending on the level of competition. The competition is divided into three levels: Novice, which is on leash and has a course that uses only 10 to 15 stations; Advanced, which is off leash and uses 12 to 17 stations, three of which are considered "advanced" maneuvers, and a jump (a broad jump, high jump, or bar jump); and Rally Excellent, also off leash with 15 to 20 stations, a minimum of three advanced level exercises, a minimum of two "excellent" level exercises, two jumps, and the honor exercise. During the honor exercise, the dog must remain on leash on a long *down* or *sit-stay* while another dog runs the Rally Excellent course.

Attend a Rally Event. See how the finished product works, how dogs enter the ring, and how handlers interact with their dogs, and get a feel for the event and the amount of polish you and your Boxer need to participate—and perhaps even place in your class. (Many videos are posted on YouTube, too. Use "rally obedience" as search words.)

Work on Basic Skills. Walking nicely on a leash is a good start with working toward a more formal *heel*, in which the dog's shoulder does not surge past or lag from your left hip. *Sit*, *down*, and *stay* are all skills to work on while searching out an obedience club that offers Rally classes.

What It Takes for Rally

- Any and all Boxers. Challenge your puppy or find a new activity for your elderly Boxer—or any and all ages in between. Rally is really for everyone.
- Enthusiasm. This sport is meant to be fun, and titles are attainable by all dogs.

Exercises include changes in pace, spirals to the left and right, jumps, about-turns, and figure 8s.

Three qualifying scores of 70 points out of a possible 100 under three different judges are required for a title.

Getting Started

Find a Rally or Rally-O training club. This sport requires stations and a knowledge of what each exercise is. The signage is in "shorthand" and is necessarily self-explanatory to the first timer.

Schutzhund

Though perhaps mostly known for the protection segment of the test, Schutzhund is a sport that includes much more, including competitions and titles in endurance, obedience, tracking, and Schutzhund itself, which is a three-part test of obedience, tracking, and protection work.

Schutzhund is *not* a means to train a protection dog; it is only a sport and should be taught using positive reinforcement and play training. Those who seek

Schutzhund sport because they feel unsafe in their homes think that this training will provide protection; however, they'd be better off installing an alarm system in their homes. If the protection portion of Schutzhund is taught correctly, the Boxer will only bite the arm of a "bad guy" if he is wearing a special protective sleeve. This is because this sport is taught as a sport only, and uses play-based training. In order to get a Boxer to bite and hold onto the "helper's" arm in competition, the dog is taught to play tug with the padded sleeve. He has no intention of hurting the person wearing the sleeve. In fact, if you were to give a properly trained Schutzhund Boxer the command to "bite" someone who didn't have a sleeve on, he would be very confused. It would be very much like telling your Boxer to fetch a ball when you hadn't thrown anything.

Not every Boxer has the correct skill set to be competitive in the full, three-part Schutzhund competition. Dogs that excel in obedience, tracking, *and* protection work often come from proven working Boxers lines and possess much higher play drives than most pet Boxers. However, Schutzhund training clubs offer the obedience and tracking segments as individual competitions, too, allowing Boxers and owners of all levels and drives to have fun and compete.

Getting Started: Schutzhund

1. **Find a Play-based Training Club.**
   This point cannot be emphasized enough. There are some clubs in North

America that still employ harsher training methods. To find a quality training club that is Boxer-friendly, consult with USA-BOX for suggestions for training clubs in your area.

2. **Look for a Boxer-savvy Trainer.**
   German Shepherd Dogs and Belgian

Malinois dominate this sport. Their training is very different from a Boxer's. (They are capable of focusing intensely at a much earlier age, for example, and are less likely to attempt to provide comic relief for their handlers.) If you can find someone who enjoys working with Boxers, you will be that much farther ahead in training.

3. **Be Prepared to Commit a Great Deal of Time.** This sport requires many facets of training, beginning with obedience training and tracking, and finally—if you choose to participate in this area—protection work.

Scent Games and Competitions

In 2008, the National Association of Canine Scent Work (NACSW) developed a training program and competition (with four earnable titles) for "nose work." The first year saw two trials on the West Coast, but by 2011 trials were being held weekly in areas across the country. Scenting training and trials have proven to be immensely popular with owners of all size dogs. Look for NACSW trainers and trials in your area (www.funnosework.com) and other organizations offering scent games in upcoming years. Many trainers are offering "K9 Scent Games" as part of thier list of fun classes. It could just be the next big thing! And your Boxer will love it.

What It Takes for Schutzhund

- Good health and a sound body. The obedience title with Schutzhund requires jumping a substantial fence and climbing a large A-frame, among other activities. Boxers should be cleared of any health or physical problems before participating in these events.
- No aggression. With protection work, the Boxer must be self-confident, possess a stable and sound temperament, and *not* be aggressive. There is no place for aggression in this sport.

Note: If you own an aggressive Boxer, however, the trainers at a quality Schutzhund club will be skilled in helping develop a program to help you manage your Boxer, as well as train him in obedience and tracking.

- No fearful or timid temperaments.

Tracking

Both the AKC and Schutzhund clubs sanction tracking tests, and Boxers do well at both. AKC tracking tests offer three levels, which are pass/fail and are noncompetitive, and a tracking championship. Schutzhund sport offers a tracking title, as well as competition.

The only disadvantage Boxers may have with tracking is that because they are a brachycephalic breed, they do not tolerate hot temperatures well and shouldn't be asked to work when the temperatures are too high. Depending on where you live, the climate may not be a problem, or may be a concern only during the peak summer months.

In tracking, the dog must not only follow the trail left by a person through various vegetation and terrain, but he must also indicate any articles left by the person along the trail. This involves a lot of time spent training with your dog, and requires the support of a good tracking club. (This sport is definitely a group effort!)

If your dog is particularly good at tracking and attains one or more tracking titles, you might consider sharing his talents by volunteering with a local SAR team (see Search and Rescue, page 143). This public service demands a lot of time and effort; however, locating a lost person and saving a life—or even finding a body and providing closure to a family—provide untold rewards for both you and your Boxer.

Getting Started: Tracking

1. **Begin Early.** Though an old Boxer can learn new tricks, many tracking instructors recommend working on your dog's scenting abilities at an early age. As soon as he is fully vaccinated, you can begin early tracking training.
2. **Get in Shape.** Tracking is not for the weak or physically frail owner. It involves moving swiftly through potentially rugged terrain.
3. **Find a Good Training Club.** As mentioned earlier, tracking is a group effort and requires skilled training. Training with a tracking club will give you access to expert advice, as well as

training grounds where tracks can be laid and a variety of skills worked on.
4. **Keep It Positive.** Your Boxer loves to work and tracking may be the perfect sport for him. To keep his enthusiasm and enjoyment up, be sure to keep your training positive and provide plenty of rewards.
5. **Don't Be Put Off.** There are those who don't think Boxers are good working dogs. This just means they don't know Boxers. Persist and prove them all wrong.

What It Takes for Tracking

■ Good health and fitness—both dog and handler
■ Energy and enthusiasm
■ Good scenting abilities

Useful Addresses and Literature

Organizations

American Boxer Club
Website: *www.americanboxerclub.org*
Rescue listings:
  www.Americanboxerrescue.org/
  boxersitesrescue.html
Questions:
  abcquestions@americanboxerclub.org

American Boxer Rescue Association
  (ABRA)
Website: *www.americanboxerrescue.org*
P.O. Box 184
Carmel, IN 46082

United States Boxer Association/USA-BOX
Website: *www.usboxer.org*
Questions: *usboxerclub@gmail.com*

Boxer-Klub E.V. Sitz München
Veldener Str 64+66
81241 Munich, Germany
011 49-89-54670812
Website: *www.bk-muenchen.de*
  www.boxerKlub.de

American Kennel Club (AKC)
AKC Customer Care
8051 Arco Corporate Drive, Suite 100
Raleigh, NC 27617-3390
(919) 233-9767
Website: *www.akc.org*

United Kennel Club (UKC)
100 E. Kilgore Road
Kalamazoo, MI 49002-5584
(269) 343-9020
Website: *www.ukcdogs.com*

Activities/Behavior

Agility
AKC (See Organizations above.)

Agility Association of Canada (AAC)
Website: *www.aac.ca*

Canine Performance Events (CPE)
P.O. Box 805
South Lyon, MI 48178
Website: *www.k9cpe.com*

North American Dog Agility Council
  (NADAC)
HCR 2, Box 277
St. Maries, ID 83861
Website: *www.nadac.com*

UKC (See Organiaations.)

United States Dog Agility Association
  (USDAA)
P.O. Box 850955
Richardson, TX 75085
(972) 487-2200
Website: *www.usdaa.com*

Animal-Assisted Therapy
The Delta Society
875 124th Avenue NE #101
Bellevue, WA 98005
(425) 679-5500
Website: *www.deltasociety.com*

Therapy Dogs International, Inc.
88 Bartley Road
Flanders, NJ 07836
(973) 252-9800
Website: *www.tdi-dog.org*

Behavior
Animal Behavior Society
402 N. Park Avenue
Bloomington, IN 47408
(812) 856-5541
Website: *www.animalbehaviorsociety.org*

American Veterinary Medical Association
1931 N. Meacham Road, Suite 100
Schaumburg, IL 60173-4360
(800) 248-2862

Canine Good Citizen
(See American Kennel Club listing.)

Conformation
(See American Kennel Club listing.)

(See United Kennel Club listing.)

Deaf Boxers
Deaf Dog Education Action Fund (DDEAF)
P.O. Box 2840
Oneca, FL 34264-2840
E-mail: ddeaf@deafdogs.org
Website: *www.deafdogs.org*

Flyball
North American Flyball Association (NAFA)
1400 Devon Avenue, Box 512
Chicago, IL 60660
Website: *www.flyball.org*
(800) 318-6312

Obedience
(See American Kennel Club listing.)

(See United Kennel Club listing.)

Association of Pet Dog Trainers (APDT)
101 N. Main Street, Suite 610
Greenville, SC 29601
(800) 738-3647
Website: *www.apdt.com*

National Association of Dog Obedience
  Instructors (NADOI)
P.O. Box 1439
Socorro, NM 87801
(505) 850-5957
Website: *www.nadoi.org*

Rally-style Obedience
(See American Kennel Club information.)

Rally
(See APDT information under Obedience.)

C-Wags
3693 Fairview Avenue
Jackson, MI 49203
Website: *www.c-wags.org*

Canadian Association of Rally Obedience
Website: *www.canadianrallyo.ca*

Schutzhund
DVG America
Website: *www.dvgamerica.com*

United Schutzhund Clubs of America
3810 Paule Avenue
St. Louis, MO 63125
(314) 638-9686
E-mail: usaschutzhund@worldnet.att.net

(See United States Boxer Association/
USA-BOX listing under Organizations.)

Search and Rescue
American Rescue Dog Association
P.O. Box 151
Chester, NY 10918
Website: *www.ardainc.org*

Tracking
(See American Kennel Club listing.)

(See Schutzhund listing.)

Books

Activities

Agility: Simmons-Moake, Jane. *Agility Training, the Fun Sport for All Dogs.* New York: Howell Book House, 1992.

Animal-Assisted Therapy: Davis, Kathy Diamond. *Therapy Dogs: Training Your Dog to Reach Others.* Wanatchee, WA: Dogwise Publishing, 2002.

Canine Good Citizen: Volhard, Jack and Wendy Volhard. *The Canine Good Citizen: Every Dog Can Be One*, 2nd edition. New York: Howell Book House, 1997.

Conformation: Coile, Caroline D. *Show Me! A Dog Show Primer*, 2nd edition. Hauppauge, NY: Barron's Educational Series, 2009.

First Aid: Heath, Sebastian and Andrea O'Shea. *Rescuing Rover: A First Aid and Disaster Guide for Dog Owners.* West Lafayette, Indiana: Purdue University Press, 1999.

Flyball: Olson, Lonnie. *Flyball Racing: The Dog Sport for Everyone.* New York: Macmillan General Reference, 1997.

Obedience: Bauman, Diane. *Beyond Basic Dog Training*, 3rd edition. New York: Howell Book House, 2003.

Schutzhund: Barwig, Susan. *Schutzhund: Theory and Training Methods.* New York: Howell Book House, 1991.

Search and Rescue: American Dog Rescue Association. *Search and Rescue Dogs: Training Methods.* New York: Howell Book House, 1991.

Tracking: Mueller, Betty A. *About Tracking Dog Training: Creating a Problem Solving Partnership.* Fanklin, NY: Howln Moon Press, 2008.

Behavior/Training

General Behavior: Burch, Mary R. and Jon S. Bailey. *How Dogs Learn.* New York: Howell Book House, 1999.

Coren, Stanley. *How to Speak Dog*: *Mastering the Art of Dog-Human Communication.* New York: The Free Press, 2001.

Fogle, Bruce. *The Dog's Mind*: *Understanding Your Dog's Behavior.* New York: Howell Book House, 1992.

Behaviors (Problem): Pryor, Karen. *Don't Shoot The Dog! The New Art of Teaching and Training*, 3rd edition. Ringpress Books, 2006.

Clicker Training: Pryor, Karen. *Getting Started*: *Clicker Training for Dogs*, 4th edition. Waltham, MA: Sunshine Books, Inc., 2005.

Deaf Dog Training: Becker, Susan Cope. *Living With a Deaf Dog*, 2nd edition. Cincinnati, Ohio: Susan Cope Becker, 1998.

House-training: London, Karen B., Ph.D., and Patricia B. McConnell, Ph.D. *Way to Go! How to Housetrain a Dog of Any Age.* McConnell Publishing, 2003.

Index